Faith and Five Dollars

Five dollars, six countries, four months and a one way ticket to Southern Russia. This is a book about faith, obedience, and miracles.

By Jonathan Nowlen

"Everybody wants a miracle; we just don't want to be in a situation where we need one. You can't have one without the other. Sometimes what we perceive as our problem is really God setting us up to do something miraculous in our lives. It's about training ourselves to see those problems as opportunities so God can intervene."

— *Pastor Mark Batterson*

"Expect great things from God and attempt great things for God."

— *William Carey*

Faith and Five Dollars

Copyright Jonathan Nowlen 2014
All rights reserved.

All scripture quoted from the NASB unless otherwise noted.

This book is dedicated to my amazing parents, Andrew and Carol Nowlen, who set the course of my life towards knowing God and making Him known.

Special thanks to Michelle Presley for great editing and sacrificially investing in this project!

Table of Contents

Chapter 1 ~ Into the Fire   1
Chapter 2 ~ Looking Back   9
Chapter 3 ~ Do You Trust Me?   17
Chapter 4 ~ Miracles and a One Way Ticket   26
Chapter 5 ~ Back in the USSR   33
Chapter 6 ~ Into Action   47
Chapter 7 ~ Stepping Into the Unknown   59
Chapter 8 ~ Journey of Faith   72
Chapter 9 ~ Nothing "Normal"   88
Chapter 10 ~ Miracle in Minsk   94
Chapter 11 ~ The Great Escape!   104
Chapter 12 ~ The Watermelon War   115
Chapter 13 ~ Onward to Israel   128
Chapter 14 ~ Five Dollars   132

Introduction

The story I recount in this book takes place in the early 1990's when I was in my twenties. As I write, I am now 40 years old and have lived through dozens more similar experiences in my life and ministry in over 60 countries. I would not be where I am today if I had not been willing to trust and obey at a young age. My goal with this book is to inspire the reader to truly know the Lord and to learn to hear and obey His voice.

So many Christians go through life bound by feelings of inadequacy, unable to "perform." It is my hope that my testimony will inspire you to see beyond what the wisdom the world sets forward as valuable and even what the "religious world" endorses as the right way to go about a Christian life. I want to inspire you to live and work from a place of God's favor rather than for His favor.

I believe I was able to thrive in this experience because I didn't know any better. I had not yet heard that God does not move in miraculous power, or that He does not speak to people any more except through the Bible. So I was ready to believe whatever He said!

I am grateful that I had an opportunity to meet the Lord in the realm of the impossible and put myself in a position where He could prove Himself to me. It is my prayer that this book will lead you into the waters of impossibility and will motivate you to learn how to swim.

One more thing: In this book I am recounting a story within a story. As you read, you might wonder what else was going on in the ministry aspect of the work we were doing. However, my focus is on the story within the story. In life there is, "What's going on" and then there is, "What is really going on." This experience taught me to see my reality and circumstances through the eyes of the Lord and to gain heavenly perspective so that I would be able to see what is really going on.

2 Cor. 4:18
"...while we look not at the things which are seen, but at the things which are not seen; for the things which are seen are temporal, but the things which are not seen are eternal."

Chapter 1 ~ Into the Fire

Our train ride from St. Petersburg, Russia to Riga, Latvia was surely about to end with jail time. We were flying along the rails on a vintage soviet-era passenger train that we had boarded the day before. This was supposed to be the easy leg of an already mystifying and life-shaping trip that had consumed the better part of the previous 3 months of my life. My team consisted of a band of young mission workers who had met and trained together in a mission training center during the previous year. We also had met a few mission workers in St. Petersburg who had been working in Russia, and who joined our team there.

Our team had been formed through the invitation of our team leader, John. John had a vision, and a network of contacts in Russia as well as in a number of other former Soviet Republics. Our mission was to undertake follow-up discipleship training camps with the young people who had become Christians during recent, large-scale evangelistic crusades.

St. Petersburg in those days was, and still is, an incredibly beautiful and intriguing city. However, these were dark days in the former Soviet Union. Law and order was in short supply; mafia factions controlled virtually every aspect of the economy; morality was unknown; life was cheap, and God was a concept that needed a lengthy explanation. We were relieved to escape the dangerous environment of the city. Our team had just completed an amazing time of ministry with hundreds of young Russian believers and those who were just on the edge of coming into the Kingdom. This had been our first stop on this nearly three-month journey that would see us serve in St. Petersburg, Russia, Latvia, Belarus and back again to Krasnodar in southern Russia.

Although this particular train trip had begun simply enough back in St. Petersburg, the first sign of pending trouble became apparent shortly after the train began to pull out of the station. As our train slowly picked up speed heading into the beautiful, lush, green countryside, we had all begun to relax in our rooms on the train. We were fortunate to have purchased tickets for comfortable sleeper cars and we were all looking forward to a good night of rest and recovery from our fruitful but very difficult camps.

To give you an idea of the type of stress we were recovering from, it may be helpful to recount the unexpected details of our arrival into St. Petersburg. On arrival, we found ourselves in a small minibus racing through the streets of the city. We were crammed from floor to ceiling in this van, ten people riding high on top of all our luggage. We couldn't help noticing that our local contacts were extremely nervous during this crammed commute, and, moreover, that they seemed to resent our very presence there.

However, when we pressed them for the reasons for their nervousness, we discovered that we were not the object of their consternation. As we pulled up to a large, uninviting, five-story grey building, our driver first stopped across the street to survey the entrances to the building and watch for any suspicious vehicles that may have been parked nearby. We kept quiet and watched this unexpected development take shape. Once our contact was convinced that the coast was clear, we pulled forward into an alley that was on the back side of a Christian ministry center. As we pulled up next to the back door in the alley our driver sharply warned us not to stop moving or let anyone see us when we exited the vehicle. Our contact quickly explained that he was very afraid we would be spotted and immediately become targets for kidnapping or robbery by the local mafia factions. He pulled up next to the door and slid the minibus side door open. We quickly piled out and into the building with all our luggage. In the early 1990's this part of the world could easily be compared to the wild-wild west. However, we made it through our short stay at this ministry center without any issues, managing to stay unnoticed until our departure.

As our train now sped along, our train car attendant began making her way through the car checking everyone's tickets and looking over passports. She was a nice enough middle-aged lady, abnormally happy and good natured as compared to my more frequent, previous experiences with stout and surly women who tended the cars on Russian trains. As she handed me back my passport she proceeded to kindly inform me that we should pack our belongings because we were going to be arrested at the Latvian border!

Needless to say, this ruined my moment of rest and relaxation. John, our team leader, and the rest of the group all crowded in, hoping to receive further explanation for this unexpected statement. As we all crowded around she proceeded to inform us that two weeks prior, the Latvian government had suddenly changed its rules, and would no longer issue visas on arrival at the border. Instead, visas must now be issued at a consulate outside of Latvia prior to arrival at the border. This policy change would be enforced by immediate arrest and detention of anyone who arrived at the border without a visa.

As you can imagine, this was really not good news. Half of our group had acquired their Latvian visas in the USA prior to arriving in St. Petersburg for the first leg of our trip. The other half of the group, including myself, had all been in Russia already for the previous 2 months and were not aware of the rule change. These were the days before all things could be known with a simple check of the internet. Once you were on the field you were largely disconnected from usual sources of information. These days, with the advent of widespread internet access, it is almost impossible to be disconnected from your home country or social circles. In the early 1990's in this part of the world it could cost up to $60 per page to even send a fax, if the opportunity to do so existed at all! (Does anyone born after 1993 even know what a Fax is anymore?)

Fear quickly began to set in. Facing imminent imprisonment for obeying Christ can offer a formidable faith challenge to even a veteran believer. Our group created a plan to limit the number of team members who would face arrest. We split the team into two groups: in one compartment were those with visas, and in another were those without. We decided to pretend that the two groups, located each in its assigned train compartment, were not associated with each other. In so doing, we hoped that only the members of the group who lacked visas would be detained, while the other half of the group would be admitted to Latvia. I found myself putting on layers of extra clothes, stuffing candy bars into my pockets, jars of peanut butter into my cargo pant pockets, hiding my few dollars of cash in my sock. I was convinced that we were going to be living the high life stuck in a jail cell on the Latvian border indefinitely. I would learn later how close that was to the truth. As Mike and I were frantically organizing for incarceration, I looked over at one of the ladies on our team. She was relaxed, stretched out on her train car bed. She looked at me with obvious irritation and said, "I'm not even going to put my shoes on. We are not going to jail." I didn't have that level of confidence, and my fears were soon confirmed. By this time it was the late evening and we had just begun to approach the border of Russia and Estonia.

It is important to note that at this stage of the dissolution of the Soviet empire, Estonia was more or less a no-man's land, with no functioning government or working borders. Russia, on the other hand, maintained their side of the border and all other borders, with large numbers of bored and visionless soldiers.

On our team, we were privileged to have a young Latvian mission worker who had actually trained with me in my original mission training program. We had become friends during our missions training program and she had joined our team for the trip from Russia back to her home town in Latvia.

She spoke not only, Latvian and English, but she also spoke fluent Russian, as most Latvians did at that time. As we approached the border and the train was coming to a stop, she said, "Don't speak to me in English."

At this point, we experienced what was to become a regular border crossing ritual for the first time. The train stopped and squads of soldiers began entering each train car. We could hear them coming down the train car, pounding on doors and demanding to see documents. There was a tremendous amount of yelling, arguing, scuffles and occasionally individuals or entire families who had document problems would be tossed off of the train in the middle of nowhere, even at night! Those of us who did not have Latvian visas waited nervously, along with our Latvian friend, for the imminent showdown with the border guards.

As anticipated, they began pounding on the door of our train compartment. Three guards with machine guns at the ready pushed into our tiny room and demanded our "papers". Our fears were being realized, and we hadn't even reached Latvia yet! The guards demanded our passports and were not amused to find that we did not have Latvian visas. These guards had no English language ability, and began to demand that our Latvian friend communicate to us that, "we were now to be thrown off of the train," in the middle of nowhere, in the middle of the night. All of us understood enough Russian to catch the essence of what was being communicated. Our Latvian friend began to pretend that she was not able to speak English, and that she couldn't figure out how to tell us the verdict. The soldiers became extremely agitated and an argument about our fate followed. After 10 minutes of this intense encounter one soldier finally said, "Forget about them! Let them take their chances with the Latvians!" And, just like that, they walked away and we were through! Nevertheless, our trouble at the Russian border was just the beginning.

One of my favorite statements of scripture is the second part of *Daniel 11:32b. NKJV "... but the people who know their God shall be strong, and carry out great exploits."*

This scripture was beginning to really come alive in my life as I found myself in the middle of this God-story. When I embarked two months earlier, I had no idea how this four-month mission trip would shape my future and lay a foundation for future faith exploits.

Chapter 2 ~ Looking Back

I had grown up in a wonderful Christian family. My father was a pastor and church planter in Montana in the early 1970's. He and my mother answered the call to the mission field when I was barely five years old. They sold everything, packed up the kids and left on one-way tickets to the Pacific to serve with a mission organization.

From a very young age I was deeply spiritually aware. One of my earliest memories from my fifth year of life was a season of spiritual conflict that began during my parents' missions training program in Kona, Hawaii. We lived on a large campus where many missionaries were involved in discipleship and missions training courses. In my childlike perception, it was a long walk between where we ate, where we lived, where I attended kindergarten and to other events on campus. I distinctly remember becoming aware that when I and my family returned home to our small studio apartment each evening, there were dark spirits lurking up on the exposed rafters of our apartment. Strangely, fear was not my reaction to this experience. I somehow had discernment in my young heart, and knew that these spirits intended to harm my parents. I could feel their hatred every time we entered. A holy anger and zeal began to rise up in me when I faced these spirits. One day, I decided that I was not going to tolerate this situation any more, and I was going to do something to protect my parents from these evil spirits. So, returning home one day, I ran as fast as I could in order to get into the apartment before the rest of my family. My aim was to confront these enemies and make them leave our apartment. I burst into the apartment and started yelling at the spirits that I could see them and that they had to get out of our apartment! They were startled and panicked when they realized I could see them and that I was confronting them. I was so angry and so determined to rid our apartment of these creatures that I made an effort to follow this same routine each time we returned home. Finally, one day after my latest confrontation, the spirits left and did not return to the apartment any more. I'm not sure what my parents thought was going on, or if they thought I was having a childhood meltdown, but I seem to remember them listening to me try to explain why I was yelling.

I was blessed to be raised in a home that had modeled true obedience to Christ at any cost. Our family went on to serve in a number of mission enterprises both overseas and in the USA. Each of these experiences were to me an, "adventure of a life-time," and taught me that faith in God is all you really need, and that God is real and His faithfulness endures forever.

My first serious test of faith and obedience as a young adult presented itself in the shape of an opportunity to venture into the former Soviet Union to conduct discipleship programs for young, new believers. I had just completed my first full year of missions training and had lived through a field assignment in Ukraine during the summer of 1993. I say "lived through" because it was one of the most difficult field assignments I've ever experienced, (and I have lived through many). As I write this I have now worked in over 60 nations and have served on hundreds of short and intermediate-term assignments. Of these, my initial field assignment in Ukraine still ranks as the most difficult, yet most rewarding, ministry experience of my life. By the completion of my initial missions training year, I had come through with powerful testimonies and a zeal to see the world reached for Christ. I had been a part of radical revival and evangelism efforts and I was ready for more. The problem was I had no plan, no money, and no apparent opportunities.

I clearly remember the moment all that changed. I was sitting at a table in the cafeteria at the campus in Salem, Oregon, quietly thinking and praying about what I was to do next. As I sat there listening for the voice of the Lord I suddenly heard another, very human voice. It was a young leader from a nearby mission center whose name was John. John walked up behind me and leaned in and said, "Do you want to go to Russia?" As I had literally just been seeking the Lord for direction I was immediately convinced that the Lord was speaking to me, so I said, "Sure, why not?"

John proceeded to invite me to join the team he was creating that would travel to Russia, Latvia, Belarus, and back to Russia during a whirlwind three-month outreach. The plan was to conduct discipleship youth camps for young people who had been reached or impacted by significant evangelistic efforts around key areas of the former Soviet Union. During those early days of openness in this part of the world, much effective evangelism was taking place but very little of even basic discipleship. Due to this, many of those who had come to know the Lord were falling away or were being recruited and deceived by cults.

Immediately after John shared the opportunity with me, I knew that the Lord was answering my prayer for direction. I was sold. I immediately began serving at a branch office of our mission that was focused on the former Soviet areas of the world. Other members of the team John was recruiting began to arrive, and we worked frantically to prepare for the huge undertaking ahead of us. One good friend, whom I met during my initial missions training phase, was a Brit named Mike. Mike also joined the team, and as we worked together, our friendship quickly deepened, and we felt ready to take on the challenge ahead.

Our leadership team identified a need for an advance team to undertake a reconnaissance mission in the southern Russian city of Krasnodar. The purpose of this advance, was to figure out how best to offer a discipleship camp and where to locate the program. When John asked Mike and me if we were up for the advance team assignment, we barely had to pause before agreeing! We had no idea what we were really agreeing to but we both had total faith in God that He would empower us and guide our steps. Although we were filled with zeal and courage, we lacked one major thing, money. I had just completed over one year of mission training programs and a three-month field assignment that had cost me literally every penny I had. I had sold my car and anything else of value I owned, in order to pay for the last fifteen months of ministry. I was broke. Mike was just as broke as I was, and he couldn't even fundraise as all of his supporters were back in England.

To compound a scheme that was already beginning to be viewed as a bit hair-brained by some of our senior leadership at the mission center, both Mike and I had the word of the Lord that we were supposed to end our trip in Israel, of all places! I had heard clearly from the Lord in a dream that we were supposed to visit the Holy-land at the end of our trip, and that same night Mike had heard the exact same thing from the Lord, in his spirit. Neither of us intended to bring it up, but somehow in the course of conversation the next day we both acknowledged this further direction from the Lord to each other. This word was a major faith-builder for each of us, and one that we were going to need to hold on to in the face of huge challenges to come. So we proceeded to let our senior leadership know that in addition to our already unfunded four-month trip, we were supposed to somehow make it to Israel on our way back to England. Praise God for the value the training and culture of our organization placed on hearing and obeying the voice of the Lord! Our leadership listened carefully as we told them about our new, previously unplanned stopover in the Middle East, and told us, "That's great! We will get back to you with our decision regarding whether or not to approve this." To their credit, they actually took us seriously and considered this additional direction. They were already somewhat unconvinced about our initial plans to do the four-month trip since we had no money whatsoever, and had let us know that, "our ducks were not in a row."

As the approval process dragged out, we finally realized that they were not likely to agree without additional prompting. We knew we had the word of the Lord and we needed to find a way to convince them! So we began combing through a number of books that were written by and about our current leadership. One of these books actually detailed an account of unparalleled miracles and radical obedience, featuring some of our current leadership sneaking into the Soviet Union while it was still a closed country, and engaging in amazing ministry opportunities and wild adventures with The Lord. These accounts were so extreme that our leaders had to use false names in the accounts to protect their identities! We decided that if God allowed them to obey and serve in such radical opportunities, that we also should be given the same chance. So we bookmarked key passages from this book and took it into a meeting with our senior leadership. We proceeded to respectfully point out the far more risky enterprises that they had undertaken at our age, all the while respectfully calling them by their "false" names that were used in the book. This slightly humorous approach worked! The following morning we found a post-it note on our office door that just said, "Go for it, guys." God doesn't need your ducks to be in a row. He is order, and can order the ducks any way He chooses. We now had the official commission for this assignment but we still lacked a major component: money.

Our team leader, John, still believed by faith that something would work out for us to depart early, and to be able to organize the discipleship program in Southern Russia. Our plan was to spend the first 8 weeks on this initial assignment, and then to meet up with John and the rest of the team in St. Petersburg, Russia. We had no idea what we were getting ourselves into. I really believe that often the reason God does not paint a clear and long-term picture for our lives is that we would see the artwork and say, "No way, I'm not doing it!" It's better that He reveal only our next steps, like a painter revealing a painting one brush stroke at a time. The sign of someone who truly knows their God is that they know that He is trustworthy and faithful. This person can step out and obey even when it seems like they are stepping off of a cliff! In doing so, they find that God makes straight their paths and honors their obedience.

The time was quickly approaching for our departure to Russia. Mike and I were increasingly excited for the opportunity ahead, even though we had no idea what to expect. A last-minute development in our plans was that we were also to escort a young missionary named Faith. Faith was heading to Russia for a one-year assignment in Krasnodar, but had decided to join our team on this four-month outreach prior to beginning her commitment on the field. We soon began to joke that God had given us a prophetic reminder of what would be vital for this trip by giving us a friend and teammate named Faith. The events ahead could only be described as a continuous miracle. None of us could have anticipated what we would see the Lord do in us and through us.

Chapter 3 ~ Do You Trust Me?

I was not what the traditional Christian world would have called a top-tier candidate for foreign mission work. Looking back on this experience and my early days of serving on the mission field, I can echo many great men of God who have said, "God doesn't call the equipped, He equips the Called." It seems true that all God really is looking for is availability and obedience. The Bible makes this clear in 2 Corinthians 12:9 when Paul says:

"And He has said to me, 'My grace is sufficient for you, for power is perfected in weakness.' Most gladly, therefore, I will rather boast about my weaknesses, so that the power of Christ may dwell in me."

I am comfortable with this scripture. I always believed it was ok to not be God's "number-one choice." I am convinced I was somewhere back down the line of desirable candidates, but God was able to make His grace sufficient for me and allow His power to dwell in me. My qualifications were that I was willing and available, and I was consumed with the Kingdom of God. Despite my long hair, terribly unfashionable clothing and exotic jewelry, inside, the place where God sees us, I was deeply committed to Jesus and consumed with Him, His Kingdom, and His Glory.

It soon became apparent that even my senior pastor in Salem, Oregon, had little regard for, or understanding of, my life and calling in missions. After returning from my initial field assignment to Ukraine in the Summer of 1993, I had been invited by my college pastor to share some testimonies from my recent experience on the field. As I shared a few highlights from the trip with the whole church my college pastor jumped up and added, "Jonathan has preached to tens of thousands, and many thousands have come to the Lord though his ministry." I hadn't told anyone besides him about the scale of the revival we had been privileged to be a part of in Ukraine. Truly, thousands had come to Christ and many were healed and delivered in that outreach. As my college pastor made this statement to the church, I could see my senior pastor's face staring at me in disbelief. He was muttering over and over the words, "I never would have guessed."

From my outward appearance at the time, any average Christian leader would have labeled me as, "Not that guy, he's not the number-one choice." Although I knew at the time that people viewed me this way, and I knew that it was largely due to my questionable fashion choices and hairstyles; I also knew that inside I was consumed by the Lord. Later in life when I met my beautiful wife, Robin, I realized that all those years of fashion atrocities where just God's plan to keep me from any chance of getting married until I met my perfect match! All things work together for the good of those who believe, and are called by His name, right?

I believe I connected with the heart of God for the lost for the first time when I was 16 years old. I was standing on a balcony in Ukraine, overlooking a completely lost, unreached city. It was 1990 and the wall had just fallen in Eastern Europe. I was traveling with a team of teenagers ministering through Eastern Europe, Ukraine and Russia for the Summer. As I stood on this wall overlooking the city, I was mesmerized watching all the people swarming the streets. As I watched, my heart began to break and I began to weep quietly. All I could think was to pray out "Oh God, what can WE do?" Looking back, this quiet prayer, "What can WE do?" is what changed everything. No longer was the world's condition someone else's problem, or God's responsibility alone. My spirit was willingly being fused to the purposes and plans of God by stating that WE needed to do something. Not just, "God you need to do something." I really believe that God took me up on this prayer, and together WE began to do something. I found that the things that were burning on God's heart began to burn into my heart like a branding iron and I was never the same.

So God had clearly called me to do this impossible outreach. With man things are impossible but with God all things are possible. I was one week away from departure, and I still had no money. Mike had a return ticket to England and no funds beyond that. I needed a round trip flight to England and then Mike and I additionally needed to fly from England to Krasnodar, then on to St. Petersburg; then by train to Latvia, to Belarus, to Southern Russia; after that we were to fly to Moscow, then to Israel and back to London. In addition, we needed funds for food and housing along the way. Only God could do this for us.

What happened next began a series of Miracles that quite literally shaped the rest of my life. Although our team went on to accomplish much good and effective ministry during this wild adventure, the sub-plot of God's intervention that I observed throughout my experience, overshadows even the ministry we worked so hard for. The sub-plot I observed was the hand of God moving mountains to show His faithfulness to those who would hear and obey.

The first sign of God moving the heavens on my behalf was a phone call. A call rang into our office and one of my team members handed me the phone. To my complete surprise it was one of my former high school teachers on the line. I had not spoken to this particular teacher since shortly after graduation, but he was aware of my mission endeavors through my regular newsletters. As this particular trip had come up suddenly and I had not sent out communications about the trip yet I was surprised when the first thing he asked me was, "Do you need money?" I knew he was a Christian, and I knew that he wasn't someone who would joke about something like this. No greetings or pleasantries, just the question, "Do you need money?" When I didn't immediately answer, he went on to say that he had just inherited money from a relative unexpectedly, and God had spoken to him clearly and said, "Give Jonathan $700 dollars." So in an act of impressive obedience he had immediately called me. When he mentioned the exact figure of "$700 dollars" I knew that the hand of the Lord was at work right before my eyes. The fact was that I needed exactly $700 to purchase my round-trip flight to London, and this sum would be just enough to also purchase a one-way connection from London to Krasnodar in Southern Russia.

A week earlier, I had gone to a travel agent and reserved the flight I needed to London and had also booked the one-way flight into southern Russia. I reasoned that I would book the minimum flights required to accomplish what I believed the Lord had set before me to do. The travel agent was justifiably skeptical as we completed the booking. She said, "I'll sell you this itinerary only because I know that worker from your organization always make it back somehow." She made it clear that she was technically not supposed to sell one-way tickets into Russia: especially not into a volatile region like Southern Russia.

So when I received this call from my former teacher, who had received the word of the Lord to give me $700 dollars, I couldn't respond for a minute as the exactness of the dollar amount sank in. Of course, I said, "Yes," I needed the money! I told him, "Hold on, and I'll be at your house in 30 minutes." At this point in our waiting for the provision of the Lord, the faith of even our stout-hearted team had begun to waver regarding whether or not Mike and I would actually make it on this assignment. I borrowed a car and raced over to my former teacher's home to pick up the check. I only had one hour to get to the travel agent in order to complete the purchase for my one-way flight to Southern Russia. It was then 4pm on Friday afternoon, and the travel agency closed at 5pm. My flight was scheduled to depart on Monday, from Seattle. In addition, we had to begin driving to Washington state early on Saturday morning, because we were scheduled to help Faith pack for her departure to Russia.

As I raced to the travel agency I suddenly realized what I was about to do. I was about to head into Southern Russia on a one-way flight, completely cut off from support, phones, or communication, and with no local, on-the-ground support. In addition, I had no money to live on, much less to complete this over four-month assignment. We didn't have credit cards in those days, and even if we had, no one in Russia would have accepted them. There were also no ATMs, few functioning banks, nor any other means of accessing money once you were there. You only had what you carried in with you. So if I arrived there with no funds, I would have no way to get any money unless God sovereignly provided.

As I drove across town I heard the Lord clearly say to me, "Do you trust me?" "Do you trust that if I'm able to get you there, I can get you back?" I did trust Him, and I told Him so. After this exchange with the Lord, the thought crossed my mind that I should stop and call my parents to let them know what I was planning to do. They knew about the upcoming trip, and also that I had no money. I stopped to use a phone to call my mom. I explained what I was planning to do and what I believed the Lord had said to me. As a veteran missionary herself who had done equally crazy things, (and with three kids), she really couldn't oppose the plan. All she said was, "That's nice honey. We don't have any money to help you out, so if you get stranded somewhere, don't call us." I actually had to laugh out loud when she calmly made this statement. There wasn't going to be a way to call anyone from Russia anyway! So I rushed off and made it to the travel agency with 15 minutes to spare. I hadn't even had an opportunity to cash the check from my teacher before I arrived at the agency, so the travel agent actually let me sign the check over to her on the spot to pay for the flights! It was exactly enough. I left the travel agency with only hours to pack and get ready to leave the next morning. God was just in time and with just enough.

One of the life lessons I learned during this experience was that God is looking for people who are willing to go "all in" to obey Him. So many times in our lives we pray things like, "God use me," or we make statements like, "I want to reach the world for Christ, and complete the Great Commission." While these are noble prayers and right responses which flow from our passion for the Lord, we often are not willing to do what needs to be done, or to take a step of obedience when it seems that step may take us off of a cliff. The principle I have learned over the years is that the Lord is honored when we are willing to at least fall in the right direction when He leads us to step out. Most often, the proverbial ducks never do line up. Sometimes the ducks of that old American adage even seem to get under your feet and trip you up! Go as far as you can in the direction you were called with whatever God provides.

Sometimes, as I learned on this outreach, there doesn't appear to be any provision. That is not, and cannot be a reason not to obey when you know Him who has called you. If you truly know Him personally it means that you have experienced Him and know the truth about His good and faithful character: that he will never leave you or forsake you. He is the Good Shepherd and He always leads you to the green grass and provides for your life and your soul. If you have not ever allowed yourself to be put in a situation where there is no other option than to put your trust in Christ completely, not just for salvation, but for your very life, you are missing out.

You have to invite this quality of a walk with God, especially if you come from a developed country and have the means at your disposal to fortify your life. The world's system seeks to misuse wealth for the purpose of building a safe and predictable fortress around a vulnerable existence. Each of us has a built-in desire for safety and security. The problem arises when we allow the deep needs of this inherent instinct to be met by material securities rather than by the faithfulness of God. Moreover, material security can easily become a manifestation of distrust in our Lord, an indictment against His character, and a disbelief of the promises in His word.

Chapter 4 ~ Miracles and a One Way Ticket

Saturday morning arrived, and we drove to Washington state, en route to our flight to England. I left for Washington with only $20 in my pocket. I don't think I told even Mike that I had such a small amount of money with me, and with no way to obtain any further funds. Often, God chooses not to work or provide in the ways that we would expect. He is faithful but not predictable. My initial thought as I headed up to Washington was that God still had a couple days to miraculously provide for my needs. I don't think I had given much thought to the idea that I might not see the anticipated provision immediately. In fact, by the time Monday morning came and we were dropped off at the airport in Seattle, I had already spent $15 of my $20 dollars, and so was down to one, measly, five-dollar bill in my pocket.

Our flight to England was uneventful. Upon our arrival, we stayed at the home of Mike's mother in Ipswitch, England. Mike's mom was wonderful. She graciously took care of us and housed us. This was to be the first of many future visits and transits through England as I made my way to some far-off location in the world. We jokingly began to call her home, "The Ipswitch Center," in honor of our regular stays.

Meanwhile, however, Mike and I were facing a real challenge. While I had at least been able to purchase a one-way flight to Krasnodar in Southern Russia, Mike had yet to secure any funding or flights from England onward. We had a few days scheduled in England before we, or at least I, would have to fly on to Russia to begin our work there. I was out of ideas. For now, at least, I was stranded in England, in a nice home, and was provided with food to eat. I had no money even to ride the bus anywhere, but at least I was comfortable. As the days passed, and our departure drew closer and closer, it became clear that there was no apparent way for me to obtain the sum of money I needed for this trip.

I wasn't feeling spiritual or prayerful at this point. My faith had already begun to wobble. Mike and I were out of ideas and this was our last day to see some kind of breakthrough with finances. In the morning we decided to spend our last hours of opportunity playing video games. Again, I didn't say that I was probably God's first choice for this mission. I was just willing to obey. The scripture clearly says that God uses the weak and foolish things of the world to confound the wise. I was truly feeling weak and foolish that day, and video games were actually helping to cheer me up.

As we put our video game skills to the test, suddenly Mike sat up and declared loudly, "I've Got It!" "Got what?" I asked. "I'm going to ask the bank for the money!" I didn't even have a frame of reference for such a statement. Mike went on to explain that he felt compelled from the Lord to just go down to the bank, talk to the manager and ask for the capital we needed for our transportation costs. My low level of faith really showed at this point. I told Mike to go ahead and talk to the bank; I was going to stay and play video games. To me this sounded like a last minute, desperate move that had no chance of success. Be careful what you doubt. Mike took off in a rush, since the bank was going to be closing in a few hours and he would need to to travel there by bus. After he had acquired the funds, he would then need to get to the travel agent, again by bus, before 5pm! At least, this was how it was all going to work out in his plan. So mike ran off to catch the bus while I continued to hone my gaming skills at his house.

I was starting to get worried. It was already past 9pm, and Mike had neither contacted us, nor turned up at the house. If his plan actually worked, we would have to be ready to depart in the morning. Just when we were starting to get really worried, Mike burst in the door soaked with rain, and yelled, "I got the tickets!" I was in complete disbelief.

Mike's bizarre story began to unfold as he told us that he showed up at the bank and asked to speak to the bank manager, who was a family friend. Unfortunately, he encountered a problem right away, because the manager who knew Mike was gone, and another, new manager was covering his position. So, Mike sat down with this new bank manager and gave the situation to her straight. He told her what our mission was, that we needed to leave in the morning, and that we had no money. He wanted the bank to give him the money right away so that we could purchase our necessary flights and train tickets today. He was so convinced that the Lord had given him this plan that it didn't even seem strange to him to sit down at a bank and make this request. He explained to the manager that he was planning to attend Oxford in the Fall term, and that he would then be doing fine financially, and would pay the loan back without issue at that time. To his great surprise, after he had completed making his case to the manager, she just looked at him for a bit and then asked, "How much do you need?" He ran out of the bank and headed straight for the travel agency.

The bank had given him enough money to cover our fights to, and within, Russia and the republics, all of our train tickets, and our crazy plan to fly from Moscow to Israel, and then back to England. So all went according to his plan except for one thing. When he had finished purchasing our tickets he realized that he had absolutely no money left to purchase a bus fare back to his house. That was the reason he was so late! He ended up walking for over four hours in the rain to get back to his house with the tickets. Once again, there was just enough and just in time. At this point, we knew that the Lord was with us: or more rightly, that we were with the Lord in this.

Mike and I were riding high on excitement from the provision of the Lord when we left London for Russia the next day. Our friend and team mate, Faith, however, was not so excited about our situation. The expression, "jumping out of the frying pan and into the fire," was not far from the mark. We were heading to a remote area of Russia for nearly two months, and we had no money to live on. In fact, our situation had become even more complicated at the last minute. We had originally planned to stay with a missionary family in Krasnodar and had anticipated that they would be able to help us live, adjust and learn to function. They were our only contacts in the region, because there were not many Christian workers in that region during that time period. However, shortly before our departure, we received news that our host family had to suddenly leave the area. So we were facing the reality that we had no local help at our location. The family said we were welcome to use their home and that they would leave it unlocked. They didn't know if they would be returning in the future or not. They were just glad to have someone stay in their place while they were gone.

This situation was concerning for all three of us. None of us had been to Russia before, nor did we know how to live or function there. Mike and Faith each spoke a little bit of Russian, but I was brand new to the language. As Mike and I talked about our situation, one significant concern came up. Faith was a compassionate girl, and we were both concerned that if she discovered how broke we were, she might, out of compassion, offer to pay for our living expenses. If she did this, she would be spending part of the provision that God had given her to live on for the rest of the year in Russia.

As I mentioned earlier, there were no ATM's and few banks from which to access any additional funds. Whatever you carried in with you, was all you possessed. So, while on the flight to Russia we decided to set some ground-rules to avoid this potential situation. We told Faith, "God got us into this. He has brought us this far, and He is going to provide for us. We won't allow you to spend a dime on us out of your own money. God will provide." After we made our case with her she reluctantly agreed to this plan. However, toward the end of this long flight, she suddenly spoke up and told us that God had just spoken to her. God had made it clear to her that if she was willing to take a risk and would cover the living expenses for Mike and me during our time in Southern Russia, then He would repay her ten times for whatever she spent on us. Now it was her turn to make her case to us. She explained the new ground rules and told us that she was going to be paying for our living expenses and that we were not allowed to argue with her about it. Faith was absolutely convinced that there would be a ten-fold return on her investment. We were not allowed to refuse her offer, and in so doing, mess up the arrangement God had made with her. So then it was our turn to reluctantly agree. Our standing joke at that time began to be the statement, "Living by Faith," quite literally!

Southern Russia proved to be a huge challenge and also a blessed time of ongoing miracles.

Chapter 5 ~ Back in the USSR

When we landed in Krasnodar we begin to realize how solitary we really were. Our immediate quest upon arrival was to find the house where we were supposed to stay. Russia was a country struggling to stand on its feet after decades of decline during the soviet era. Everything was difficult. It was often difficult for the population to even obtain the basic needs of survival. Transportation was unreliable and severely overcrowded. Food was almost unobtainable, and water had to be boiled before drinking. Even if you had money, there were no restaurants nor any bottled water to purchase. Stores carried very little besides canned sardines, salty cheese, and sausages. No one spoke English in these days in the outlying parts of Russia.

We had obtained a hand-written set of instructions outlining bus numbers and the number of stops to expect on each connection. Without the ability to ask directions effectively in Russian it was going to take a miracle for us to find our house. Finally, we believed we had identified the correct stop and got off of the overloaded bus. Most buses were severely overcrowded, to the point of providing absurd comic relief for us during even the hardest days of survival in post-Soviet Russian society. The average bus was designed with a capacity of about

60 or 70 people to sit and stand. The usual load, however, was often in excess of 300 people! The buses would actually drag their rear bumpers on the pavement due to the excessive weight. Under these circumstances, public transportation was a difficult undertaking even if you knew where you were going.

We made it to what we believed was our neighborhood and headed down a shattered road with trash fires burning on all sides. We showed our address to an old lady who was walking a tiny lap dog and she was able to point us in the general direction.

The house in which we were to stay for the next two months was a small, pre-World War II home, constructed with the typical corrugated cement roof panels. As soon as we arrived at the house we closed ourselves in and felt that we should pray to remain "invisible" in both the natural and spiritual realms. Russia was dangerous in those days, especially for westerners and for Americans in particular. Most of the society was either lawless or controlled by local mafia factions and strongmen. There were very few options for the people to earn a living in those days. Almost all of the men were involved to some degree in the black-market, or worse. There was very little hope of any protection from the local police who mainly kept their uniform and position just to make money from giving out bogus traffic tickets that were "payable in cash on the spot." What is certain is that the Russian government never saw much of the money from those alleged violations. From the time we arrived, we felt the fear on the streets. You never knew who you could trust or who would kill you just for the fun of it. It could be corrupt police, drunken military or local mafia thugs who would abuse you, or worse. We quickly learned a new dimension to the scripture that we were to be, "wise as serpents, but innocent as doves."

One situation that may give a sense of how desperate the times were, especially for young men, was our friend Sergei's situation. Sergei was just seventeen years old and had become a dedicated Christian at about fifteen years of age. I became friends with Sergei after meeting him regularly at church on Sundays. One day, when we were sitting in church together he began to weep uncontrollably. I proceeded to try to find out what was causing his grief and all he could say was, "I have big problems with the mafia in my family." Later, he explained to me why he couldn't attend our discipleship camp later in the summer. He said that his father was a big-time mafia boss. Sergei was compelled under duress to act as one of his father's enforcers and to translate for black market deals between the Ukrainian mafia and other European mafia factions. Each year, they spent much of the Summer months in Southern European cities arranging deals. Sergei felt desperately trapped. If he refused to assist his family, they would either kill him or turn him in to the police, along with evidence of his "crimes." I prayed with Sergei many times during our two months together, but after he departed for his trip to Southern Europe we never heard from him again. Russian society was broken and desperate at this period of history. My heart was constantly breaking for the people all around us who we learned to love and care for.

Fortunately, our small house was tucked away amid overgrown trees and bushes that kept it virtually invisible from the front. This was a great advantage, as no one could observe us when we came in and went out.

Without local support, we were in for a tough time regarding even our basic survival, much less our ability to accomplish any ministry tasks. We had two primary objectives beyond just finding food to eat each day; we had to find a way to connect with, and recruit, brand new, local churches to partner with us to send their students to our discipleship youth camp; and we had to make our way to the Black Sea region to find a secure a camp location.

Most of our first month was also filled with diligent language-learning efforts. Although my Russian language skills were coming along fairly well, that didn't keep us from making epic language errors that brought regular amusement and outright fits of laughter from people at the market where we frequently shopped. One of the most memorable humiliations at the market happened when I attempted to order two kilos of bread flour, but due to a slight misuse of intonation, I accidentally ordered two kilos of pain and torture instead. The ladies standing behind the counter in the market progressed from stunned and confused looks on their faces, to literally rolling on the ground behind the counter, howling with laughter, and pointing at us while trying to catch their breath. We had no idea what we had done to bring on this explosion of laughter. This episode went on for at least fifteen minutes, to the point that we had to give up on buying flour and move on to other shopping attempts. When we got home later that night we used a Russian / English dictionary to discover our linguistic mistake. When we understood what we had said, we laughed for at least three days! Needless to say, we were famous at the market from then on. When we arrived to do our shopping, the ladies behind the flour counter saw us coming, and before we could get to the counter to order, they had already begun to fall on their hands and knees in uncontrollable laughter. We finally concluded that we had at least imported some regular humor with which to relieve the dismal environment that was the open market in post-Soviet Russia.

God truly honored and answered our prayer for "invisibility". We felt irrationally safe even though each day was full of necessary risks and unknown situations. By the end of the first month we had begun to make progress toward our goal of inspiring local churches to support the vision of discipleship youth camps. Commitments were starting to materialize. This is when the devil decided to push back and to push back hard. We were making progress, and apparently were becoming a threat to the enemies' plans and his strongholds in the area.

The attack came in a completely unexpected way. I had grown up as a spiritually sensitive child, living in environments around the world where spiritual warfare and demonic activity often crossed the lines between the invisible world and the visible world. When the attack came, it proved to be one of the most bizarre and life-changing experiences that had ever happened in my life.

Ephesians 6:12 says *"For our struggle is not against flesh and blood, but against the rulers, against the powers, against the world forces of this darkness, against the spiritual forces of wickedness in the heavenly places."*

Most Christians in the west are so sheltered by positive and secure church and family environments that they rarely experience full-force demonic attacks, much less those that cross over into the physical and visible world.

This is testimony to the victorious and sanctifying work of Christ, who is steadily redeeming and sanctifying our spheres of influence and responsibility in countries that are heavily populated by people who love the Lord.

However, Russia in these early days of post-Soviet freedom was far from influenced or spiritually subjugated by the blood of Jesus. Evil was largely unchecked and the new Christian churches were just beginning to understand their spiritual authority and the power of the Holy Spirit. Somehow, we were discovered spiritually and the shield of "invisibility" that we had prayed for was compromised.

The way our small house was arranged only allowed for one actual bedroom. Mike and I ceded the small back bedroom to Faith and he and I slept on the living room floor. That night as I lay on the floor of the living room trying desperately to fall asleep I could not settle my soul enough to rest. Mike was instantly asleep and fortunately missed out on most of the bizarre events that followed. As I lay trying to will myself to sleep I began to pray. I distinctly heard the Lord tell me that He was keeping me awake because something was about to happen that I would need to deal with. This didn't settle my soul at all.

Suddenly, I began to hear Faith cry out in her sleep from the back bedroom. She began to yell out in a confrontational way, but I could tell she was actually still asleep, as she slurred her words and didn't get sentences out clearly. I began to think that I should start praying for her when, unexpectedly, as I lay on my back staring up at the dark roof of the living room, the ceiling began to move. Slowly, the whole ceiling and the upper part of the living room walls began to spin in a clockwise direction. It was like being inside the base of a slow-moving tornado. As this happened, I could begin to make out shapes and faces in the swirling darkness. I was struck with instant alarm and fear. All I could think to do at first, was to not let the enemy see that I was awake and aware of what was going on. "Just don't move, and keep your eyes mostly closed, and they won't notice you," I kept telling myself. The veil between the spiritual and the natural realms had been pulled back, and God was revealing to me that the enemy had descended on us in a brazen attack. I wasn't at all sure what the outcome of this situation would be.

After my initial fear and alarm, my spirit became suddenly aware that I needed to act. I felt a distinct impression that the only thing that would save us was to call on the name of the Lord. I was not at all sure what to say or how to say it, but I knew I had to try. I knew that the minute I spoke out I would be noticed, and that the whole supernatural melee that I now found myself in the midst of would immediately focus itself on me.

All I could think to do, was to say, "Holy Spirit, I invite You here." I knew from many previous spiritual conflicts and encounters that the power of God and the name of Jesus are more than enough to rescue us from any reckless spiritual attack by the enemy. All I could think was that somehow the enemy was overplaying his hand in this attack. How could he not know that the servants of God would call on the name of the Lord and be saved?

So I began to speak out and invite the Holy Spirit. It produced the most amazing and magnificent result! I only got out the words, "Holy Spirit, I..." The Holy Spirit did not even wait for the whole prayer and invitation, but exploded into that house like a Holy hand-grenade. A blinding white flash erupted in the living room and blew apart the swirling darkness that was engulfing the ceiling of the room. As a warm glow and powerful peace filled the room, I heard the very loud sound of frantic, clawed feet trying desperately to get traction on the roof and flee. It was like the sound of a terrified poodle on a hardwood floor that is trying to suddenly sprint for its life, but can't get traction. The sound of flailing claws on the roof and the subsequent racing thumps of feet on the roof caused me to almost cheer out load at the terrified retreat of the enemy and for the greatness of our God! With loud and distinct thumps, evil spirits jumped from the roof and landed in our back yard. Neighbors' dogs began barking frantically and I could hear the sounds of fleeing demons as the dogs all started barking along the route along which they fled, until they were so far away that I couldn't hear the dogs anymore. We were saved both spiritually and physically by the explosive invasion of the presence of the Holy Spirit.

Immediately, Faith calmed down in her sleep and quit yelling out. Complete peace descended on the house and I easily fell asleep thinking to myself that all I had to do was to invite the presence of the Lord, the precious Holy Spirit, and I would be saved from any weapon that was formed against me. This experience was a life lesson like no other. I realized I had nothing to fear, no agents of the kingdom of darkness could stand in the presence of the Holy Spirit. The Bible says in 1 John 4:4 *"You are from God, little children, and have overcome them; because greater is He who is in you than he who is in the world."* What a powerful truth.

The real joy I experience in retelling this epic story of faith and obedience motivates me to share this account. As I have gone on to serve in various countries, in all manner of charitable and Christian efforts around the world, I continue to long for the miraculous. Our lives are short and frail. I don't want to waste time and energy that should be used for the cause of Christ on things that are just good ideas.

There are a million good ideas available for the average Christian. There is no shortage of noble and sacrificial enterprises that can be undertaken through various churches, agencies and non-profits. The real question that has to be addressed is, has God asked you to begin this action, or did your own compassion and response to human need motivate you? Freedom, joy and miracles accompany obedience to Christ. Notice I didn't say ease, worldly wealth, comfort or happiness. In my experience, the things that need to be done in the kingdom are currently not being done, precisely because they are not fun or even emotionally rewarding.

In obedience to the word of the Lord you find freedom: freedom in knowing that this was God's idea. When it is God's idea you are free from wondering if you made the right decision to get involved. You are free from doubt, free from fear of failure, and you can always fall back on the word of the Lord when things get difficult. I can guarantee you that anything you take on that falls into the category of advancing the Kingdom of God will encounter significant difficulties. I also say joy is a by-product of stepping out on the word of the Lord. The Bible says that the joy of the Lord is our strength, and we need strength.

Joy comes from recognizing and realizing who you are in Christ. If you truly understand your identity as a son or daughter of the King, and that you are seated in heavenly places with Christ, you can not help but sense your heart jump for joy at this revelation. I believe the joy becomes your strength when you realize that God is going to do something powerful in you and through you as you step out and obey. In my own life I have often felt a complete and deeply rooted joy flow out of me when facing the worst situations. Often, I have found myself laughing out loud when in the middle of a difficult or dangerous situation that has arisen out of my choice to obey. I have begun to realize that this reaction is my spirit rising up in joy to strengthen my flesh and soul. It wasn't that the situations were humorous, but that my spirit saw my circumstances in clear perspective next to the person of Christ. To my spirit, every adverse circumstance seemed laughable in comparison to the power of God.

The role of the miraculous that rises up to show the power and favor of God when you obey cannot be emphasized enough. There are different levels of obedience, and I believe that they produce different types of outcomes in a person's life. It's easy to "obey" when all the ducks are in a row, you have a ten-year strategic plan, and all the resources you need are lined up like a crack team of professional athletes. Anyone can choose to "obey" in those circumstances, and rightfully should obey. The challenge of this storyline is that it rarely presents itself in real life, and even when your options do look like the best-case-scenario mentioned previously, this will present a few challenges of its own. I would question the appearance of a best-case-scenario for the following reasons:

Why is there no tangible resistance from the enemy?
Any kingdom undertaking that is of God will by definition be against the enemy, and he and his forces will push back to try to hold on to what they think is their terrain.

Is this undertaking something that I could do in my own strength?

If God left the project altogether, how would I notice? We have to be ok with things in life requiring God-sized intervention to succeed.

Am I allowing room for any of the miracles that God can do and wants to do on our behalf?

I read a quote from pastor Mark Batterson who once said "Everybody wants a miracle; we just don't want to be in a situation where we need one".[1] I could not agree more!

---

[1] Jessica Martinez, *Pastor Mark Batterson: Everyone Wants Miracles but Not the Situation That Requires One (Christian Post: Church and Ministry: 2014),*
http://www.christianpost.com/news/pastor-mark-batterson-everyone-wants-miracles-but-not-the-situation-that-requires-one-125409/

The most memorable parts of my many ventures in the Kingdom have been those aspects in which God has turned the impossible into the possible through acts of power and wisdom that could only come from Him. I honestly don't remember much of what has gone "well" by human standards in the past. What I remember, and what I believe heaven remembers, are the times in which I obeyed, and the Lord rescued and saved through His mighty hand. He rescued and proved himself when I had no power or ability to accomplish what I was being asked to do. In these types of situations, we give God the pen and paper and He writes the script. Often to our discomfort, He writes the script as we go along, testing our faith and our confidence in His character.

If we allow ourselves to be put into these kinds of "obedience moments" in which things don't make sense, the ducks are not in a row, and even the wisdom of friends and family may be against our choice to obey; if we still hold on to the word of the Lord we begin to see miracles. I don't know about you, but that's all I want to see at this point in my life. God is not impressed with our great knowledge, experience, wisdom or talents. God is impressed with the person who obeys and holds nothing back; with the one who goes "all in." He is impressed not with conditional obedience, but with unconditional obedience: with the one who hears and obeys.

Chapter 6 ~ Into Action

Now that we had spent over a month learning the Russian language, networking with local churches and finding agreement with our vision for the discipleship camp, we faced the next phase of our assignment. We had to research and locate a suitable facility that would be able to host our program later in the summer.

You must understand the nature of such an undertaking in post-Soviet Russia. The country and many of its facilities were in shambles. Everything was falling to ruin, having emerged from a failed system. Not only was the country physically falling apart, but also, the condition of the population was dismal as well. Not a day went by in which God did not allow our hearts to be broken for the countless situations of hopelessness and loss that the people were experiencing. Nothing can prepare you for immersion in a culture that has had the very life and soul ripped out by oppression and sin.

To give you an example of the spiritual destitution of many of the young people in those days, if you told someone, in all sincerity, that God loved them, they would respond with, "What is a God?" Not, "Which God?" or, "Who is God?" or, "I don't believe in God," etc. They actually had no idea what a "God" was. As I shared about the Lord, I often found myself beginning with explanations about the very idea of a "God." It was heartbreaking. Nevertheless, to see the spark of salvation lead to a flame of fire that restored their souls, was worth every bit of hardship one faced in the process.

Our quest for a camp location took us to the far southern city of Tuapse on the coast of the Black Sea. This coastal city was accessible by bus from Krasnodar but was still very isolated, and very few foreigners were entering that region during this time. This excursion started out with a bang, quite literally. On arrival, we stayed in an apartment with another missionary. The apartment was tiny, and I found myself sleeping out on an enclosed balcony that hung three-stories above the street below. That first morning, I was jolted awake by a massive explosion on the street below. Someone had thrown a hand-grenade at a passing car, and the explosion had literally gone off just below the balcony I was sleeping on. My ears were ringing, and the explosion had severely jarred my body, even through the floor that I was sleeping on. What a way to start the day! I stumbled into the main apartment living room holding my head and trying to fully wake up. Our host was up, along with Mike and Faith.

The missionary we were staying with proceeded to educate us briefly on the social conditions that were were walking into. We learned some startling information. The mafia was largely in control of the city and the region and nearly everyone was involved in some form of criminal activity. He proceeded to explain that they had done some polling in the local grade schools in the course of teaching the children. These polls asked the basic question, "What do you want to do when you grow up?" 90% of the boys indicated that they wanted to join the mafia and 70% of the girls indicated that they wanted to become prostitutes! When asked why they had given these answers, the students said, "These are the only things you can do to make money." To make matters worse, it was very common for the parents of high school aged boys to force them to commit a serious crime, in order to have something to hold over the head of their own child. These families would tell their sons, "If you try to leave the mafia we will turn you over to the police along with this evidence of your crimes." The social fabric was coming apart at the seams.

We proceeded to make our way from Tuapse out to a small, coastal village that we learned had previously operated a Soviet Youth Camp. Russia, along with the other, former Soviet republics, were scattered with youth camp facilities. It was, and still is, a cultural expectation for students to go away for weeks or months during the summer to these camps. During Soviet times, the camps served as indoctrination centers, in which students were molded, and their characters were solidified, making them good, contributing members of the state. Following the dissolution of the Soviet Union, these camps continued to operate, but became marginally-organized recreational experiences for students. Many of the camp facilities had deteriorated greatly with the loss of government funding. They were therefore eager to rent out their facilities for an international youth camp.

In this village, we resided with a very amusing Russian family who had become Christians quite recently. They spoke fairly good English, and were able to help us negotiate a deal to use this local youth camp for our program.

After we had successfully completed negotiations, the father of the house made me a surprising offer. He pointed out across the field behind the apartment complex, to a visible military base. Indicating a very large attack helicopter parked on the tarmac, he asked me if I wanted to go for a ride! He was a military pilot, and that was his assigned helicopter. Of course, I agreed! Who would turn down an opportunity like that? As I prepared for the ride of my life in this helicopter that was straight out of a cold-war thriller, I found out the bad news… the local Russian military was insolvent, and the helicopter was therefore out of gas. What a let-down! This was the pilot's only free day, and the gas truck was late.

My consolation prize was an invitation on the following day to see him conduct military training exercises along the coast line. He was flying a large load of young, Russian soldiers, who were training to parachute out of a helicopter over the ocean, with the goal of landing on the beach. Of course, I said, "Yes!" to this invitation too.

Mike, Faith and I found ourselves at the beach, watching as this helicopter climbed to a very high altitude. Soldiers began falling out of the open side door of the helicopter and pulled their chutes open immediately. Then it all became surreal. The wind began to blow in all different directions, and the parachuting soldiers were blown back over the ocean, away from the beach. These guys were heavily loaded with equipment and weapons and had no plan for landing in the water. Soldiers began landing all around us as tanks and heavy vehicles sped all over the beach conducting maneuvers. All I could think was that I would never have had an opportunity to be in the middle of this in any other country and, "I almost got a ride in that chopper." The drama continued as about a dozen of the solders landed in the surf and deeper water. What began as an an exercise, turned into a massive rescue operation to fish out of the water soldiers who were struggling to stay afloat while wearing all of their gear. Miraculously, no one died. This experience again added credence to our regular comment that, "there was never a dull day in Russia."

After that, we headed back to Tuapse for another day before we needed to get back to Krasnodar. I really believe we don't know the half of what God and His guardian angels save us from on a regular basis. Every once in awhile you go through an experience and realize afterwards that only the hand of the Lord could have saved you.

A war was on, and we had no idea. In those days in Russia you had to watch CNN to find out what was happening a few miles away from where you were. There was no local media and no source of news other than either rumors, or newspapers that were brought in by people traveling in from another country. Therefore, we had no idea what was going on in our own immediate area of Russia, much less the rest of the world. We found out the hard way that Russia had just gone to war with Chechnya and that we were mere miles from the front line. We had begun to notice an abnormal number of fighter jets flying in formation toward the South, but didn't think anything of it. As it turns out, they were in full combat mode and on their way to support a massive ground war that Russia had engaged with Muslim radicals in Chechnya. Not only did we not know there was a war on, but we decided that on our last day in Tuapse we were going to visit a local beach to enjoy the sun for awhile. We had a great time and had no idea what a dangerous situation lay ahead.

Around dusk, we began walking back through the city toward our apartment. All of a sudden, a squad of military police began to walk along the road parallel to us, and slowly moved to intercept us. As they began to draw close, Mike and I could see that this was trouble. They walked up beside us and then began to separate us from one another as we continued walking. Mike whispered to me to not let them know that I spoke any Russian, and then we were too far apart to communicate anymore. The commander of the squad walked up beside me, and put his arm around my shoulder as we continued walking up the street. He and the other military police were eyeing us and evaluating us as we went forward. This commander began to speak to me in Russian. He said, "Show me your passports." I didn't have my passport with me because I had left it at our apartment, and, I absolutely did not want these guys knowing where we were staying; so I pretended not to know what he was asking. He continued, and asked, "Who are you? What are you doing here? Don't you know you are in a war zone?" He was asking these questions in a very intimidating manner, and I was beginning to become unnerved. I could tell these questions were leading up to something and was beginning to feel that these military police were viewing us as serious violators of some form of Marshall Law that had been established.

We continued walking up the street, pretending to not understand the gravity of our situation. The commander made the shape of a pistol with his hand and put his fingers up against my head and said, "I could shoot you right now and no one would ask any questions." Now I was concerned. These guys were in full intimidation mode and we had no way of knowing whether they were serious or not. These are the times when you have to fall back on the word of the Lord: that He got you into this situation and He is going to get you out.

The Lord did intervene to save us again from an impossible situation. As we approached the end of the street, along with our "captors," we arrived at a major intersection. Suddenly, the commander who, moments earlier had been threatening my life, stopped and said, "This is the end of our patrol zone." We stopped too, not knowing what they expected of us. The Commander's demeanor suddenly changed and he began laughing out loud. He said, "Forget all of that! Come with us, and let's go get drunk together!" Talk about a turn of events! We felt that this was our window of opportunity to just walk away, so we politely turned down the bizarre offer to get drunk with a surly bunch of Russian military police, and quickly headed up the steep city streets toward our apartment. We took a few roundabout routes to make sure we were not being followed, and gratefully arrived back at our apartment in one piece. The Lord had delivered us once again.

Later that evening we told our host about our encounter with the military police and to our surprise he wasn't very interested in that situation, but instead wanted to know which beach we had been to. We explained to him the location of the beach we had enjoyed earlier that day. He exhaled deeply and said, "You are lucky you left when you did." He went on to explain that this beach was called, "Sniper Beach." We had no idea of the risks at this beach. However, looking back, we had wondered aloud why almost no one was visiting this beautiful beach. The beach overlooked a large port, with many merchant and military ships moored at the huge docks. Apparently, the beach got its name because, after sunset, Russian military snipers positioned on ships across the harbor would shoot at anyone they saw on the beach! "Why in the world would somebody do that?" I asked, shocked, and suddenly very aware of another near miss that the Lord had delivered us from.

Our friend told us that there was so much mafia activity and pirating going on in the harbor, staged from that beach, that the military just assumed that anyone there after sunset was up to no good. The military had a simple solution. Just shoot anything you see on the beach. What a crazy world we live in. After hearing about our second close call that day were were glad to be moving on from Tuapse in the morning.

Psalms 68:20 says, *"God is to us a God of deliverances; And to God the Lord belong escapes from death."*

Our God is able to deliver us from the plans of the enemy and from the schemes of evil men. As this scripture tells us, many times in our lives we have come close to death but never realized it because of God's care and deliverance for us. His care and deliverance is part of His character and nature. At times in our lives, we find ourselves in situations which require God to deliver us. In these situations we are well aware of our weakness and need. Understanding the character and nature of God actually reshapes our thought patterns and, in turn, shapes our willingness to trust God. When I speak about the need to "know God," this is the kind of insight to which I am referring. We have to develop a deep understanding of who God is: His nature, character and ways.

God has created us in his image and likeness for the purpose of relationship. God created us in such a way that we could know Him and He could Know us. God is knowable. He has orchestrated all of creation and the fullness of His written word to reveal himself to us.

Romans 1:20 says, *"For since the creation of the world His invisible attributes, His eternal power and divine na-*

ture, have been clearly seen, being understood through what has been made, so that they are without excuse."

What has been made, all of creation, is pointing out the character and nature of God. If you know God and are familiar with His ways, you are willing to obey even when you feel that you are stepping out into the unknown. This is where your peace comes from.

Peace emanates from a conscious awareness of the character and nature of the God who created you and loves you. Peace is not the absence of problems but the presence of God. Someone might ask, "How do you come to know the, "Ways of God?" In my life experience, one can only really begin to know the ways of God if one is able to observe them.

One way that we observe His ways is through study of the scripture. In one of my favorite ways to read through the Old Testament, I focus on and observe only the ways in which God relates to the various characters in the text. One can begin to see recurring patterns of preferences, deferences, likes, dislikes, and what moves the heart of God. Once you have established this type of baseline observation through scripture then you have a grid through which to interpret the spiritual events you face in life. The second way we learn to know the ways of God is through walking closely with Him through the paths of impossibility in life. On these paths, God is the only one with the answers and the power to pull us through and prosper us, even in the valley of the shadow of death.

The Bible says in Psalms 23:5, *"You prepare a table before me in the presence of my enemies; You have anointed my head with oil; My cup overflows."*

This is a good example of one of the, "ways of God." He provides you with abundant provision even as you sit in the presence of the enemy of your soul.

One of His ways that we can grow to understand is that He often allows us to find ourselves in a very unsettling proximity to the devil and his evil plans for our lives. But we realize if we know the ways of God that he also chooses this very moment to shower us with abundant provision and affirm our calling in the heavenly realm.

Knowing the ways of God enables us to anticipate in faith what He will do, even if we find ourselves facing an insurmountable situation. You can even begin to look forward to difficult situations if you are able to see your circumstances through the lens of His character, nature and ways. There is a significant difference between knowing about someone and knowing someone. We must spend considerable quality time with someone if we want to truly know them. In the same way we must spend quality time with the Lord on a personal level if we hope to truly know Him.

Chapter 7 ~ Stepping Into the Unknown

Our miraculous story continued as we headed back to Krasnodar. It was almost time for us to move out of our little, hidden-away house, and fly to St. Petersburg to join the rest of our team. We couldn't believe so much had happened in two short months. As this was the first time any of us had been sent out on an assignment like this, we were amazed at how the power and purposes of God could be accomplished through such unlikely people. One of my favorite life scriptures has been, and still is in Corinthians where the apostle Paul refers to us as weak and foolish things. Even now, after two decades of full-time Christian service, I still realize that it is only the power of God working in me and through me that accomplishes these kingdom purposes.

Paul says in 1 Corinthians 1:27, *"But God has chosen the foolish things of the world to shame the wise, and God has chosen the weak things of the world to shame the things which are strong."*

Praise God that He chooses us and makes us wise and makes us strong in Him!

Some people ask me, "How do you feel confident or able to handle these very risky situations?" God speaks to this clearly in His word through the apostle Paul when he says in 2 Corinthians 9:8, *"And God is able to make all grace abound to you, so that always having all sufficiency in everything, you may have an abundance for every good deed."*

If a person has survived their walk in the impossible, or we could say, "in the valley of the shadow of death," they usually come to the realization that they in themselves are not sufficient. God can and does provide all sufficiency, in everything, "for every good deed." Don't let feelings of inadequacy hinder you from obeying and stepping out in faith. You will find that God is happy to choose the weak and foolish things of the world and make them sufficient. This is how the world often sees the Glory of God expressed. God receives all the glory and praise when people see very average people accomplishing above average things that are far beyond the reach of their own strength or ability. Allowing yourself to live as a conduit for God's greatness makes you a living testimony to the power and nature of God.

Over the years I have often, if not most of the time, found myself responsible for ministries or efforts that I was never really trained for or prepared for. Often, these situations and leadership roles were far above my pay-grade, so to speak. I chose to step out in faith and obey in these responsibilities that the Lord had set before me, and in so doing, I saw profound fruit and success that was obviously, in no way, attributable to my own skills or abilities. The outcome was always that God received the glory and praise for what He accomplished. It is a joy, and extremely reaffirming to our faith in Christ when it is obvious, even to ourselves, that only He could have done this. Praise be to God!

The next phase of our journey required a long flight from Krasnodar to St. Petersburg. This was one of the flights Mike had purchased with loan money from his Bank in England at the very beginning of our adventure. Many flights were extremely cheap in those days in the former Soviet Union. Often, a flight might cost under $100 to fly to most destinations. The only airline at that time that flew domestically within Russia and also in between Russia and the former republics, was AeroFlot.

Now, these tickets that Mike's travel agent in England had secured for us on AeroFlot were abnormally cheap. As we were not in a financial position to be choosy about our flights, we took what we could get. Not only did AeroFlot have a reputation for being incredibly cheap, but it also had a reputation for being the most dangerous airline in operation in the world. These were the kinds of risks we faced, but we were confident that the Lord would protect and preserve us. This particular AeroFlot flight put our faith to the test. As we walked out onto the tarmac toward a very large plane, we began to have some reservations. To begin with, the plane had no steps or boarding ramps up to its external doors. As we walked up to, and eventually underneath the rear of the plane, the flight attendants motioned for us to climb up a ladder that was conveniently positioned, sticking out of a cargo door near the bottom of the fuselage of the plane! We had to haul all of our luggage up this ladder system and into the cargo area of the lower deck of the plane. Once we had deposited our luggage in a pile, we climbed up some narrow stairs into the passenger compartment. Further reservations set in when we found our seats in a completely empty airplane. There was one other person, a man, sitting far up to the front of this aircraft, which must have been designed to seat 200 or more persons. The three of us sat in our own row a good distance back from the front, and looked around at this surreal situation. There appeared to be no one in charge of this plane, and, why in the world were there no other passengers on board? The plane began to taxi suddenly, and we began to laugh nervously, anticipating that something strange was afoot. As the plane took off, a roar of wind came through two of the emergency exits behind us. The plane quickly leveled off at only about nine thousand feet, and proceeded to fight its way at low speed through the dense lower atmosphere. As the plane shuddered and shook violently, we realized all of a sudden why the plane was traveling at this low altitude. The plane was not able to pressurize! No wonder the seats were less than $50! We learned later that the plane was on its way to St. Petersburg to be repaired. Then, to make matters more uncomfortable, the only flight attendant on board was an angry, middle-aged woman who forced us to accept the only drink that was available on the plane and drink it. She served us a mysterious green liquid from a silver punch bowl into plastic cups. We tried to object but she angrily insisted that we partake of this refreshment. It was awful. To make matters worse, we had previously observed her handing large bottles of Russian beer to the pilots after take-off! Sometimes, all you can do is pray and laugh. We made it to St. Petersburg three hours late due to the slow airspeed and low altitude, but we made it in one piece.

Finally reaching St. Petersburg and meeting up with the rest of our team was a mixed blessing. It was amazing to be in such a beautiful city and then to be with our team as we headed out of town to conduct a series of discipleship camps. This is what we had planned and anticipated for months! The only downside was that God had told Faith that after we left St. Petersburg, she was not to pay for our basics like food or housing any longer. So, obediently, she cut us off after we left St. Petersburg. Someone had given me $20 during our time in Southern Russia and I had carefully guarded it. I was down to about $17 of that $20 by the time I was financially on my own again. Fortunately, for the duration of the camps, our food and housing were paid for by the programs!

The camps went quite well. Our team had a lot of fun together and everyone was excited about the vision and the impact we were having in the lives of these young believers. In fact, many students who attended the camps were not yet saved, and so we had the privilege of walking with them as they came to repentance and entered the kingdom of God! We had all begun to truly love these young people with a depth of love and care that only God could produce in us. It was a love far beyond mere compassion or sympathy motivated by human need. We developed spiritual eyes to see these students the way God sees them. We began to see their potential, and to see them as Christ knew they could be: new creatures in Christ Jesus, justified, healed and completely transformed from individuals hard-wired to sin, to children of God who were hard-wired for righteousness. What a joy to see the transformation happen right in front of us! It shouldn't have been so surprising to us, but often as we grow older in the Lord we forget what we were like before we believed and were transformed.

I remember clearly when I went through this experience in my own personal salvation. When I came to Christ in full repentance and humility at the age of 13, I woke up the next morning as a very different person. One of the most pronounced changes I observed immediately in myself, was that, whereas prior to my repentance I had a propensity for, and a stronghold of anger in my life, afterward, I suddenly found that I had been completely delivered from anger and rage. After my conversion, it actually became difficult for anyone to make me angry for any reason. The day after I became a Christian I wandered into the kitchen and asked my mom if there was anything I could do to help her. She stood there shocked and asked me, "Who hit you with the Nice Stick?" I mentioned casually that I had accepted Jesus as my personal Lord and Savior last night, that was all. Obviously, I had not been prone to voluntarily offering to serve in our family kitchen prior to my conversion, but now it just came naturally. What an amazing transformation we undergo when we become followers of Christ. It was equally amazing to see the immediate re-creation of the nature, emotions and choices of these students who attended our camps.

When our camps were completed in St. Petersburg, it was time to head to Latvia, where we had scheduled three more weeks of similar camps.

Our train slowly pulled out of the tiny border station and we were able to enter Estonia. We were more than grateful and very encouraged in our faith by the way God had orchestrated our exit from Russia. We were convinced that the Lord had quietly brought us through the first impossible hurdle of the trip by bringing confusion and disagreement among the Russian border guards. They became so frustrated at not being able to communicate their initial intention of tossing us off of the train, that they finally decided to let us take our chances with the Latvians!

It was a long, late night ride as we crossed through Estonia in our classic Soviet train car. These train cars were the height of 1960's elegance. Some were in poor condition, but many were actually well maintained, and gave me the feel of being a time traveller who had found myself back in the heady days of the post-World War II communist heyday. As the train began to slow for our stop at the Latvian border, we readied ourselves and steadied ourselves for what we thought would be a certain, and short trip to a border prison.

The train seemed to slow for an eternity, creeping up to the border, and closer to our unknown fate. Finally, we came to a jolting stop at the border. We were all nervous. Quickly, we organized all team members into groups, separated into different compartments according to who had visas and who did not. All of us who did not have visas, expected to be arrested and had begun to prepare.

I had been in the Boy Scouts for a very short, yet eventful period of time. One of the things I learned there, was the Boy Scout motto: Be Prepared! So I began loading my cargo pant pockets with stashes of granola bars, fruit, and even a jar of peanut butter! I thought, "At least we won't starve..." In our room full of likely candidates for incarceration, only one, with unwavering faith, remained on her bunk bed and refused to even put on her shoes. She continued to voice her calm opinion that we were, "not going to jail." I wasn't so convinced.

Sure enough, the dreaded process began with the military boarding the train at the very front. They slowly progressed through the train cars, thoroughly checking all documents and visas. You have to give Latvia credit, they were one of the first Soviet satellite republics to really get their country back on track after the dissolution of the Soviet Union. Border security was back, law and order was being instituted on many levels, and civil society was actually beginning to function again. Unfortunately, this all materialized at the worst possible time for us. We had no idea they had made so much progress and changed so many things in the last two months!

As we sat anticipating the arrival of the Latvian military, listening intently to the yelling, screams, crashes and fighting that drew ever closer, we began to quietly pray. My Latvian friend, the girl who had been in my discipleship program in the USA, tried to encourage us by letting us know she would stick with us and negotiate on our behalf for the best possible outcome. The soldiers eventually arrived at our car, and then our compartment, and proceeded to pound on our door. As we opened the door we saw the usual formation of two men with machine guns aimed at us, and a high-ranking commander standing in between them. "Documents!" The commander barked at us in Latvian. He, along with the other soldiers, was in a seriously bad mood. The three of them had just literally fought their way down the train, and had detained many people as they enforced this new visa and entry policy. "Documents," he ordered again. We handed over our passports, and my Latvian friend began in earnest to explain our situation and plead for mercy for us. A heated and lengthy negotiation followed. I could tell things were not going well. Finally, she turned to us with her hands up in the air and said, "I've done all I can do. Now you are going to jail."

This was not the outcome we had hoped for. I remembered all of the miracles along the way on this trip, all the protection and all the provision! We thought, surely this God-story would not end with us abandoned in some remote Latvian jail. We slowly accepted our fate and gathered our belongings. "Follow me," the commander said, this time in Russian. I was the first to fall into line as we proceeded down the train car hallway behind the commander. The rest of my visa-less teammates fell in behind me and the two soldiers with guns brought up the rear. We began making our way down the hallway, headed for the door and then on to who knows what fate.

Suddenly, God intervened. The commander stopped unexpectedly, directly in front of me and spun around aggressively. He had spoken no English up to this point, and had made no effort to communicate with us directly, but had chosen instead to communicate through our Latvian friend. He still had our passports in his hand and he faced me with the passports held up in the air. In perfect English he said, "I will let you in the country, I hope they let you out!" The Commander then motioned to his soldiers to let us pass back to our compartment, and he and the soldiers quickly exited our train car. We stood there in shock. What had just happened? Our Latvian friend stood with eyes wide open and a dumbfounded look on her face. She was the first one to come to her senses, and she ordered us to move quickly back to our compartment. We got in the room and crawled into our bunks. She said, "Turn off the light, close the curtain, and don't make a sound until this train is moving!" We dutifully obeyed. We could hear the commander and the soldiers enter the train car directly behind ours, and begin the process of arresting people and dragging them off the train. There was no one but the Lord who could rescue us in the middle of such a certain fate. We were in Latvia! We had made it through a hair-raisingly close call. Once the train started moving and we were flying along the tracks toward the capital city, Riga, we started to celebrate! Needless to say, we had a considerable worship and praise time in our little train car room.

For many years after this particular incident, I wondered to myself, "Was that just a fluke situation? Maybe other people were given leniency by these soldiers too." It's hard to know in situations like these what was going on, both in the heavenly places and in the natural processes of man. Nearly five years later, I received an answer to these wonderings while in conversation with an American missionary who had worked for many years in Russia. We were in Colorado at the time of our discussion, and he had brought his family with him on this visit. There were at least five people in their family, including children. We were sitting around, casually swapping stories of faith adventures and God-stories that we had experienced in Russia. In the course of the conversation I shared with him this story of entering Latvia miraculously, without visas. He became acutely quiet as I shared the story, and then, in seriousness he asked, "When was that?" We began to figure out the details of the date, time of day, departure city, type of train, etc. Within about 15 minutes of investigation he said, "We were on that train!" He and his family had been on our very same train, on the very same night coming out of Russia and heading to Latvia. He and his family had been living and serving in Siberia for two years, and were on their way back to Europe for a furlough. He went on to explain in a somewhat agitated manner that they also did not have visas and did not know about the change in the law when they boarded the train. They had gone through the same experience we had, except that he and his entire family had been arrested and held in a Latvian jail for two weeks, beginning that very same night. He didn't know whether to be excited about what the Lord had done in delivering us from arrest or to be angry about what they had to endure! What we both agreed on was that only the Lord could have rescued our team that night if even he and his little children were detained by the same soldiers. Hearing my friend's story cleared up any remaining doubts I had as to the nature of the escape that had been provided for us on that train.

I learned that night on the train that nothing is impossible for those who are in Christ Jesus.

Chapter 8 ~ Journey of Faith

We arrived in Riga, Latvia later in the morning, and took a bus to a remote part of Latvia where a mission training center had been recently established. Now that we were traveling with a larger team again, the relational dynamic for Mike, Faith and I was changed. We assimilated back into our larger team under the competent guidance of our team leader, John. It was a breath of fresh air to be in a larger group who were pulling together toward common goals. One of the most important lessons I learned over many years of mission service in the kingdom is the importance of, "team." I credit my early experiences growing up in missions communities for my foundations of understanding the importance of teams. Serving as part of a team is hard. It is the "hard road," and yet it is the heart of God for His people.

We were all created in the image and likeness of God, and God himself, through Christ, manifested the importance of relationships, unity and laying down your life for your friends. My experiences and the wisdom I have acquired over the years have proven over and over that if you want to accomplish Kingdom purposes, regardless of the sphere of society in which you engage, you have to have a team. This principle is largely echoed in some fashion in all aspects of human existence and endeavor. One alone cannot accomplish the task.

Ecclesiastes 4:9-12 says, *"Two are better than one because they have a good return for their labor. For if either of them falls, the one will lift up his companion. But woe to the one who falls when there is not another to lift him up. Furthermore, if two lie down together they keep warm, but how can one be warm alone? And if one can overpower him who is alone, two can resist him. A cord of three strands is not quickly torn apart."*

If a cord of only three strands is not quickly torn apart, how much more a team of 5, 6 or 10, "strands?" I can honestly say that in my 20 years of full-time kingdom service in over 60 countries, I have never seen just an, "individual" or even just a, "pair" of either friends or a husband and wife, make significant headway or thrive in their mission endeavors. If you are considering stepping out in obedience to the place where the Lord is leading you, first look around you to identify those who will go with you. Who will walk with you and fight the good fight alongside you? Even the apostle Paul took along a team in the form of Barnabas, Mark and Silas, and, though not recorded, many more are likely to have come alongside Paul for certain seasons.

My advice is to focus on building a team before you step out in obedience in the direction toward which the

Lord is moving you. It is wise to make this your default setting: to find the people whose hearts the Lord is moving and calling, and then to spend quality time building your, "mobile church." In some rare cases you may be the only one willing or available to attempt some assignment for the Lord, but in my experience that is a rare occurrence. Take your time to build your, "mobile church" or, "sodality" as it is called in missiological terms[2].

There are two distinct expressions of the New Testament church that serve as helpful inspiration and validation of the one, unified, "Church," the Body of Christ:

"Modality," is the term given to the expressions of what we might call the local church. Local churches often have the distinction of being Geographically static, and therefore, ministry scope is, by default, focused on multi-generational, long-term discipleship, and cultivation of a community in the kingdom of God. The church in Corinth is a good example.

"Sodalities," on the other hand, are more like the band of volunteers who travelled with Paul the Apostle. Sodalities are distinct in that they are mobile, non-geographically static, task oriented, and involve many

---

[2] For a more detailed discussion please see the article titled 'The Two Structures of God's Redemptive Mission' by Dr. Ralph D. Winter.

specialists who are chosen or, "called" by the Holy Spirit to a season of service.

Here is one example of the way in which one might become part of the Mobile Church:

Acts 13:2-5, *"While they were ministering to the Lord and fasting, the Holy Spirit said, 'Set apart for Me Barnabas and Saul for the work to which I have called them.' Then, when they had fasted and prayed and laid their hands on them, they sent them away. So, being sent out by the Holy Spirit, they went down to Seleucia and from there they sailed to Cyprus. When they reached Salamis, they began to proclaim the word of God in the synagogues of the Jews; and they also had John as their helper."*

This small band of missionaries was formed by the, "calling" or selection of the Holy Spirit, to undertake a certain task in a certain season.

I believe that the Lord still chooses and calls certain individuals to team up as His specialists, pooling their gifts, talents and resources around a common cause that the Lord has given them. This is exactly the way in which our team came together and functioned for a season of ministry in the former Soviet Union.

Don't discount or marginalize those whom the Lord calls into the mobile church. The mobile church is just as much the, "Church" as are local expressions of the Church. Both expressions serve specific purposes in the kingdom of God and both have the same need for diverse gifts and the anointing of God.

1 Corinthians 12:21 says, *"And the eye cannot say to the hand, 'I have no need of you;' or again the head to the feet, 'I have no need of you'."*

So when you form a team to undertake an assignment from the Lord, whether in a straight-forward ministry context, or in a creative undertaking such as: forming a business that will bring hope by modeling the principles and truths of God to a hurting nation; you are the church. In the New Testament, all of the members of the Apostle Paul's team, including himself, were part of local churches. For certain seasons and assignments they became a Mobile Church, and thrived in anointing and effectiveness to accomplish the work the Lord had set before them. Much more can be said on this topic. However, for the purpose of understanding the importance of a team-based approach, this discussion should help stir your thoughts. Both local expressions of the Church, and also mobile teams, are extensions of the body of Christ, and are guided by the same Head of the Church, who is Christ.

We found ourselves staying at the new missions training center, which was located about a three-hour drive from the capital city of Riga. On the upside, we had made it into Latvia! On the downside, we had to find a way to acquire visas, or else we could face a very real demonstration of the words the Commander had spoken at the border when he said, "I hope they let you out." Getting in was one thing, but when we next attempted to leave by train, our visas would again be checked at the border, and, understandably, we wanted to avoid a situation of such intensity in the future.

Now that we knew the requirements of the new law, we set about to learn how to get our documents in order. Through much inquiry we discovered that the only way to get a visa once inside the country, was to travel to the consulate building in downtown Riga to complete an application and receive a visa stamp. We faced a number of hurdles in this scenario. First, we only had a few days to accomplish this before we needed to move to another city to begin conducting our ten-day youth camp. Second, we had no transportation, and no buses ran from the country-side where we were staying, into Riga in those days. Third, we were in the country illegally and faced the very real possibility of being arrested when we turned up asking for visas at the consulate! Our strategy was this: I would take five members of our team into Riga, in two separate groups on two separate days. This way, if the Latvian authorities decided to arrest us they would only get half of the group and not all six of us at once! This seemed reasonable, except that this plan required us to hitchhike into Riga and then back again to the remote village where we were staying, not once, but twice.

As this miraculous journey of faith continued, another lesson I learned was that God cares about both the little things and the big things that concern us. Our concerns, and the usual characteristics of life, matter just as much to our Father in heaven as do the weighty things of the kingdom of God.

Matthew 6:31-33 says, *"Do not worry then, saying, 'What will we eat?' or 'What will we drink?' or 'What will we wear for clothing?' For the Gentiles eagerly seek all these things; for your heavenly Father knows that you need all these things. But seek first His kingdom and His righteousness, and all these things will be added to you."*

Some of us on the team had begun to discuss this aspect of the ways of our heavenly Father. We had been so amazed at His timely and specific provisions for us that we had become convinced that not only did He truly want to provide for us, but also that He cared about what we cared about, even down to our personal preferences. As you draw close to the Lord in an intimate and personal relationship with Him you begin to realize that what moves you moves Him, and what moves Him begins to move you. It really does become like a wonderful marriage relationship. When a husband and wife are in a healthy and intimate marriage they become intuitive about what the other is thinking and what matters to their spouse. One of the greatest joys in a husband's married life is to successfully anticipate what will bless his wife, and to do all that he can to provide that blessing, without waiting for his spouse to ask. Likewise, a wife who is lovingly cared for by her husband will also learn what her husband is thinking and what will bless him. In our walk with the Lord, we likewise begin to be intuitive about pleasing the Lord and He also desires to bless us even when we haven't thought about a particular need or want. He knows the desires of our hearts.

As this revelation grew in our hearts we decided we wanted to put this understanding to a slightly humorous test, and we found the perfect opportunity. The day to attempt my first hitchhiking adventure into Riga arrived. We walked a couple miles through winding, single-lane, farm roads and out to a regular, two-lane highway. It was absolutely beautiful in the Latvian countryside. As with most of the former Soviet Union, there was at that time a huge disparity between those who had found a way to make money and the average citizens who still lived on Soviet-level wages, or who had no income at all. Extreme wealth and extreme poverty were the nature of the economic environment. Most of those who had wealth at that time had acquired it through illicit means, and were extremely protective of their new found wealth and possessions. Due to these social dynamics, not many vehicles travelled the roads those days, and those that were out and about were likely driven by less-than-trustworthy individuals. These were our hitchhiking options. Needless to say, some focused and concerted prayer times preceded our first attempt to reach Riga.

The three of us took up positions along the side of the road and attempted to flag down the few vehicles that passed by. The first car we spotted was a brand new Dodge Viper sports car that blasted past us at well over 100 miles per hour. Faith became frustrated at our lack of progress and said, "I'm going to pray specifically for a sports car to pick us up… a red sports car!" She was convinced that God would honor her specific prayer. Jeff, another guy from our team, and I, were not so convinced. Faith was completely convinced, though. To our great surprise, we saw in the distance a red car approaching at a high rate of speed. As it drew closer I thought out loud, "No way." It was a red, sports sedan. The driver passed us at, easily, 100 mph and then slammed on his brakes, sliding dozens of feet before coming to a stop and backing up.

We walked up to the vehicle and cautiously looked inside. It was obvious from the driver's clothes and slightly drunken demeanor that he was in some capacity involved in the mafia. I could always tell by looking at their shoes. They wore these totally relaxed workout suits, as if they lived at the gym, but then they wore a thousand-dollar pair of loafers to complete the outfit. You could tell how high up the mafia food-chain someone was by how expensive their shoes were! Under normal circumstances, we would have waived off this car after completing our initial assessment of the situation. But this time we decided it would be ok to take him up on the offer of a ride, because he had his little, five-year-old son in the front seat with him. We figured he couldn't be up to much questionable activity with his child in tow. As we entered the vehicle, we realized that his son was severely injured, and through our broken Russian we understood that the driver was on his way to the hospital in Riga to seek treatment for his son.

It was a long ride, and the driver was in an all-consuming progress mode. He was not going to let anything slow his journey to Riga to get his son to the hospital. The way he drove, we wondered whether we would need a hospital ourselves. He increased his speed, and began cruising at about 120 miles per hour, even around blind corners. We slowly and discreetly began to locate our seat belts and buckled ourselves in, thinking that there was a high likelihood that he would miss a corner at some point. There was a lot of quiet prayer going on in the back seat. Faith was convinced, rightfully so, that God had heard her prayer and had sent her the exact vehicle she had asked for, so she was not concerned at all.

The close call finally came. We were flying up a straight stretch of road when we saw a line of slowed vehicles ahead, stretching for a distance of about a quarter mile. When the road began to incline upward, our driver simply entered the oncoming lane of traffic without missing a beat, and commenced to pass the line of slower traffic. Sure enough, a Semi truck crested the horizon, headed straight toward us. By this point, there was no way that the driver could maneuver behind the line of automobiles we were passing, even if he came to a full stop, so we were fully committed to this passing process.

Faith was asleep in the middle between myself and Jeff. I looked at Jeff and he looked at me, and we couldn't believe what was happening. We were literally watching death approach us head-on, and our driver didn't even flinch. He was facing off with this Semi and was playing chicken to force the truck driver off of the road to avoid a collision. Jeff said, "Should we wake her up?" Faith was sound asleep in-between us. I said, "No, let her wake up in heaven." I could not believe the callous disregard for life that our driver was demonstrating, even the life of his own son. It was like he was suicidal on some level.

At the final second, the Semi truck veered off of the road, and roared past us in the ditch at easily over 60 miles per hour. The truck barely managed to stay upright, and then swerved back onto the road behind us. Our menace-to-society driver finished passing the slower line of autos as if nothing had happened. Jeff and I looked at each other with eyes wide! Here was another close call the Lord had delivered us from.

Our hearts were moved with compassion for our driver. These individuals had thought that striking it rich at any cost would bring happiness and meaning to their lives. However, once they arrived at their goal they often realized that they had only succeeded in giving themselves more expensive and dangerous problems than they faced before! The trap of materialism had already sprung on these young, post-Soviet men. They were often hopeless and nihilistic, becoming a reckless danger to themselves and to those around them. The only hope for this broken society was the love and transformational work of Jesus Christ.

We reached the outskirts of Riga, and as quickly as possible, exited the red sports car at the first stop light we came to. The driver didn't even acknowledge us or our hasty exit.

This was a particularly awkward moment. We walked into a large building full of complicated hallways and offices, looking for the visa office. As strange as it sounds, that was the way visas were handled just prior to our untimely arrival in Latvia: one entered the country, then visited the visa office to obtain a visa. So, knowing now that the law had changed, and that we were technically in Latvia illegally, was another test of our confidence and faith in God. If He could specifically answer prayer for the type of car we wanted for our ride to Riga, He could give us favor with the authorities in the visa office.

We found the correct office and approached the window nervously. The lady behind the glass partition asked for our passports and carefully looked through them for what seemed an eternity. Finally, she looked up at us and asked, "How did you get in this country?" I knew this was likely going to be the first question we were asked. "The guy at the border let us in," I truthfully answered. She just shook her head in disbelief. Finally, she looked up at us again, and with very serious intent said, "Don't ask for any favors." We did not. Patiently, we sat waiting in the little office seating area until she was done processing visas for us. Until she curtly handed us back our passports, we were not sure whether she was going to give us visas, or have us arrested. With a huge sigh of relief we exited that building and rejoiced at God's provision and protection! What a miracle. By this point, I was becoming accustomed to the miraculous and deeply personal intervention by the Lord throughout this faith journey. I believe God used these experiences to shape my spiritual eyesight.

2 Corinthians 4:18 says, *"While we look not at the things which are seen, but at the things which are not seen; for the things which are seen are temporal, but the things which are not seen are eternal."*

We have to be able to see beyond what is seen and what is temporal. Seeing the unseen is seeing reality through God's eyes. One sign of true spiritual maturity is being able to see what is eternal through the dominant haze of the temporal, or earthly realm. The question we need to ask ourselves is, "What do I see when I look at a given situation? Do I see through the haze and lock onto the hidden, eternal realities that are clearly visible to our Lord? Or do I only see the haze, and fixate on the difficulties and confusion of the circumstances we must navigate on this earth?" I realized as this story unfolded that God was clearly creating a life-shaping scenario that could only be truly understood by seeing every circumstance through His eyes. I began to see the miraculous when others saw only the misery and hardships. I began to celebrate the power of God when others felt like God had abandoned them. It was all about learning to let my spirit see clearly and not, "Look...at the things which are seen."

Years later, my friend Mike and I were sitting in a park in London having lunch. We were reminiscing about this particular faith journey and all of the wild adventures that had been packed into a five-month experience. By this time, I had a deep, spiritually minded understanding on every aspect of this incredible God story, yet I found that Mike did not. During our conversation I was thinking back and highlighting particular miracles and epic displays of God's power on our behalf. Mike sat thoughtfully for a few minutes and I could tell he was processing my perspective. At this point, Mike and I had not had a chance to visit each other for a couple of years, and had never found a chance to process the faith journey we had experienced together. Mike spoke up and said, "I wish I'd had the spiritual eyes to see things the way you did." Right there, I realized a real-world truth. Two people can go through the exact same circumstances, knowing and following the exact same God and Father, have the exact same resolution to an experience, and yet see the entirety of the story very, very, differently. My perspective was completely informed through the lens of the miracles of God, while Mike's was more informed by the difficultly of the various circumstances we had experienced. His general recollection was negative, and focused on the very real difficulties we had experienced. My perspective was completely focused on the chain of miracles that proved the power of God and His desire to personally guide His children through this life.

All I can say looking back many years later, is that the whole experience of your life will be shaped and viewed as either a miracle to be celebrated, or a series of cold difficulties for which you subconsciously or even consciously blame God.

Chapter 9 ~ Nothing "Normal"

There was nothing normal about this trip. Latvia proved to be just as abnormal a chapter in this God Story as anything leading up to it. We finally arrived at our camp facility and began planning and setting up for the hundreds of Latvian youth who were to attend our discipleship camp. This facility was really rough. It was a pre-World War II orphanage that was beyond derelict in its upkeep. We found ways to make-do, though. One difficulty was that there was not enough room in the building for the guys of our team to sleep inside. To solve this problem, we located the only other usable structure on the property, and set up our beds there. However, to say that we slept in, "beds," is an overstatement. We actually cleared away shop debris, wood splinters, and broken glass to sleep on the floor of an abandoned garage. It was on a par with a homeless squat house somewhere in an inner city, and nearly as dangerous. One night, some local thugs threw bricks through the remaining windows of our garage bedroom while we slept. They had mistaken us for Russians, and couldn't wait to show their animosity for the former occupying power by hurling bricks at us. Again, by God's grace, all the bricks missed us, as did the falling broken glass. The only negative byproduct was that it became incredibly cold at night without windows left to keep the heat in. Oh well, it could have been much worse.

The camp was fun, and many young Latvians became true followers of Christ. It was a blessed time of relative peace and calm for our team as well. We really needed it. It was the, "calm before the storm," as they say.

God was not about to let me get comfortable. The lessons I needed to learn along this faith journey were only beginning. Sometimes in life, when you think you have given all you have to give, there is just a little bit more that God wants to test you on. As much as we like comfort and security in our lives, these are not the environments in which we have the opportunity to grow in our trust for the Lord. Sometimes, when we are in the hardest situations, we cling to the few things in our life that give us a sense of control or comfort. In my case it was $17. Somewhere between the time we left St. Petersburg, and the end of the camp in Latvia, someone had given me $20 which was now down to $17, and I had a well-thought-out plan for that money. Even after seeing so many miracles of provision and protection along this journey, my faith was often still weak. Repeatedly, the Lord showed me that I didn't fully trust Him.

Jesus says in Matthew 6:25, *"For this reason I say to you, do not be worried about your life, as to what you will eat or what you will drink; nor for your body, as to what you will put on. Is not life more than food, and the body more than clothing? Look at the birds of the air, that they do not sow, nor reap nor gather into barns, and yet your heavenly Father feeds them. Are you not worth much more than they?"*

Even though I had read this scripture hundreds of times, I still did not have a full realization of how infinitely my Heavenly Father valued me. If I was worth enough for my Father to give His son to die in my place, how small a thing it must be for Him to provide for my daily food? This revelation came into my life deeply through an evening bible study that our team attended at a local missionary's home. This American missionary and his family had entered Latvia immediately after the fall of the Soviet Union. They had lived there through the hardest of the hard times, and it was a real honor to enjoy a meal with them and to spend some time in the Word together. During the worship time that evening, the Lord gave me a clear command. He said, "Do you trust me? I want you to give your $17 to this family." The missionary family was in an extremely difficult financial condition, and, during the meeting, John, our team leader, had felt compelled by the Lord to take up an offering from among our small team, to bless them.

This was a major internal struggle for me. I knew that the Lord had clearly told me to give my only existing money in the offering, but everything in me wanted to resist. I had plans for that money! I knew that at the end of our time in Russia, Mike and I were to fly to Israel. We still had no clarity from the Lord regarding why were were going there, or what we were going to do. Nevertheless, I had carefully planned out the use of my $17. I imagined that I might at least be able to afford to buy 1 falafel per day, during the ten days we planned to be there. At least that way I wouldn't starve, I thought to myself. What a sad and impoverished way of thinking this was, especially after witnessing the incredible provision of the Lord over the last few months. So, as the offering collection came around the room, I decided once again that I was, "all in," and that I would give every last penny in obedience to the Lord. In this complete change of attitude, I quickly threw my last remaining reserves into the offering. When I did this, I felt great peace, and a sense of the favor of the Lord flood over me. $17 had never purchased so much before.

Now I was flat broke. Sometimes people talk about being broke or penniless, but they still have access to resources. I had no money at all. My teammates were in equally bad shape. We were running on fumes, financially speaking, and most of my team had budgeted just enough to squeak by and complete this assignment. By God's grace, food was extremely cheap in those days in the western republics, if you could find it. So when I wasn't eating at the camp programs, friends on the team bought extra food and shared with me.

When this portion of our adventure was complete, we took yet another train ride. We headed from Riga, to Minsk, the capital of Belarus. This train trip was the least eventful of our entire journey. By this time we were ready for, "uneventful." Some people spend all of their free time and hard-earned money searching for adventure and thrills. I have discovered that all of those desires and more can be found in sold-out service to the Lord. The fringe-benefit is that in His service, He pays the bills and plans the ride!

I believe that deep inside every human is, not only an empty space that can only be filled by a relationship with God, but also a built-in desire for adventure, conquest, risk, nurture and beauty. This is especially evident in men, but I have seen these traits expressed in many young women as well. As I have matured in my understanding and walk with the Lord, I have come to believe that these characteristics are also part of God's character and nature. Therefore, we as beings created in His image bear these same traits. The enemy of our souls, sin, and the world's system have hijacked and corrupted these God-given instincts; but God wants to awaken and fulfill these desires in His people, through partnership with Himself, to live with passion and purpose. Sadly, in most cultures of the world, these traits and desires are only satisfied through carnal and counterfeit expressions such as video games and fantasy. So many Christians have no idea what is available to them through a true, personal walk with Jesus. I love the way C. S. Lewis describes Aslan the Lion, the type of Christ character in his famous, *Chronicles of Narnia* stories. On a number of levels, this series of books presents clear allegories of both the Kingdom of God, and also of our life experiences as human beings. In, *The Lion, the Witch, and the Wardrobe*, Aslan is described: "He's wild, you know. Not like a tame lion." This may make some people feel uncomfortable, but think of this incredible description of Himself that God forcefully communicates to Job. God says in Job 38:3-4, *"Now gird up your loins like a man, and I will ask you, and you instruct Me! Where were you when I laid the foundation of the earth?"* The rest of Job 38 is insightful into just how untamed our God really is. It is worth reading just to obtain a scriptural perspective. Yes, God is love, but He is also the God of all power and might.

Chapter 10 ~ Miracle in Minsk

Arriving in Minsk, the capital of Belarus, was an event full of mixed feelings. I was excited to be in a new republic, and looked forward to the upcoming camp programs we were to conduct. The other half of my thoughts constantly nagged at me with fear and doubts as we approached the hotel we be staying in prior to the beginning of our camps in this city. The Belarus camp location was the least researched and least known of all our programs. Belarus was in bad shape at this time. Poverty was rampant and the mafia controlled almost every aspect of life. It was a time of, every-man-for-himself thinking, that created an unstable and dangerous environment. Here we were, right in the middle of this wild west phase in Eastern Europe, and yet we were full of faith and knew beyond doubt that the Lord had directed our steps, and was making our path straight.

Our team arrived at a small hotel that was decorated in classic Soviet style. Each room contained a bunk bed, a small desk, and a chair. It was more like a military barrack or tiny college dorm room than what you might envision as a hotel room. We were just glad to be in a place with a working bathroom, and some semblance of privacy. The problem I faced was that I still had no money to pay for food, much less this decent hotel. I had literally checked into the hotel in faith that God was going to provide a way for me to pay the bill. Mike and I were sharing a bunk room and we had just begun to get settled into our tiny room when another true miracle occurred.

Now, this hotel was a wild place. It was full of random foreigners and partying mafia gunmen, and it was definitely not a place where you would want to leave your door open for very long. It was not uncommon for the perpetually-drunk mafia hotel guests who heard anyone speaking English, to force their way into a room to insist on a lively drinking party and some friendly gambling. Neither of these activities would end well for the foreigner who became so unwisely involved. On the other hand, it was also a risk to refuse these drunks, as they were the ones who were armed and tipsy. So the best plan of action was to get into the hotel room as fast as possible, close the door, and keep your voice down.

As we had closed our door, and were quietly settling into our room, suddenly there came a clear sound of something sliding under the door. I looked over, and sure enough, a small, white, envelope was laying on the floor. I quickly peeked out the door to see if anyone was in the hallway, but it was empty. On the envelope, was writing in Russian that neither Mike nor I could decipher. I opened the envelope, and to my great surprise, it was filled with Russian currency!

Now, there are a couple important facts to understand about this situation. First, none of my team members other than Mike knew that I was completely out of money. I had not let anyone know because I did not want them to feel compelled or pressured to pay for my expenses: especially since none of them had cash to spare beyond their meager personal budgets for the trip. Second, no one on our team could or would write a bunch of information in Russian on an envelope. My only surmise, was that probably, some slightly intoxicated individual had been trying to quietly pay for something illicit and did not want to be seen. Apparently, he had picked the wrong door —or, the right door— depending on whether or not you believe the hand of God was at work. By morning the next day, when no one had come around looking for a mysterious envelope of cash, it became a donation to the cause: the cause of Christ, that is. I hadn't exactly won the lottery. In the envelope, was just enough money to pay for Mike's and my hotel stay, and for the food we would need during the time we were not operating the camps. It was a spot-on amount! Not too much, and not too little. This was just another miracle in a long line of miracles that God was using to prove Himself to me.

The camp location near Minsk in which we operated our program was dismal. The facility was being used already by a regular, government-run summer camp, and really it was just summer warehousing for people's kids. We were to operate our program in a portion of the facility we had rented for ten days. Normally, we would have brought kids in from local churches or networks, but this time we directly enrolled dozens of middle school aged kids who were already living at this government-run facility. It was heart-wrenching. Every day when we arrived at the facility to begin our programs, the kids swarmed to us in a desperate crush of young people, trying to hug us and get near to us. Even little, grade school aged children would immediately hold our hands and cling to our legs. The heart-wrenching realization was that these kids knew in their spirits that we loved them and that they could trust us. We also discerned that they hoped desperately that we would rescue them and protect them from the people running this government youth camp. It became obvious that many of the children were being abused, and the agony of it for us was that there was nothing we could do to change the situation for the kids. There was no law and order, there were no police to even call. These poor kids were on their own. We spent ten days trying to bring some love and healing into their hearts and minds. All of these children accepted Christ, and many were powerfully transformed and strengthened in their hearts and minds. We spent hours and hours earnestly praying for these students, and for the conversion of the questionable supervisors at this camp facility. When the time came for us to leave, it was heartbreaking. These kids had finally found a safe place, and a family, but now we would disappear. The only one and true hope for the desperate is the power and love of Christ. We can only do so much, and we often find ourselves unable to solve the problems we see in the world. We left in prayerful tears, and I still remember those kids to this day. That experience worked to solidify my resolve to do something about the condition of the lost, and of this suffering world. It birthed in me a revelation of personal responsibility, the absolute rightness of the ways of God, and the absolute evil of the devil and world's system. I determined to fight the world's system and to see the, "Kingdom come, on earth as it is in heaven." If not me, then who?

We arrived in Minsk once again, and settled into an extremely run-down hotel near the area of the train station. We had a couple days left in Minsk before we had to take the train back to Krasnodar and then on to Tuapse on the Black Sea. With almost no means of communication, we were trusting in faith that the plans and arrangements we had organized with our local network of churches and Christians would yet hold together for that last big camp program.

After months of intense ministry, and huge amounts of physical and emotional strain, we were in great need of some rest and restoration. The schedule allowed us one free day. We soon saw that the guys and girls on our team each had very different ideas about what would constitute a restful and fun day off. The girls decided they wanted to sleep in and then do some browsing in the local street market. Not surprising. The guys on the other hand, somehow locked onto the idea that we were going to watch some soccer on TV.

Now, we hadn't even seen a television set in over three months, and we definitely did not know where to find one in Minsk. There was rumored to be a championship soccer match that was to be televised, so we focused our combined energy on finding a TV that was broadcasting the game. This pursuit became one of the most dangerous and bizarre elements to this whole adventure.

We headed out onto the streets in Minsk and began to ask all of the reasonably nice looking people we saw, where we could find a place to watch sports on TV. Oddly enough, most people pointed us in the same direction, so we were fairly convinced that somewhere at the end of this endless search there was actually a TV. We walked for miles through the city, and finally came to a series of unfinished city blocks that appeared to have been under construction at one time. The scene was post-apocalyptic. Abandoned construction equipment was everywhere, and giant construction cranes slowly rocked in the wind. There were partially-built buildings in every direction. Apparently, when the Soviet Union dissolved, this construction zone had come to a sudden stop. We asked one last person on the street if this was where we could watch sports on TV.

The area of town we found ourselves in was far from what we had envisioned. In our minds, we had imagined something like a downtown sports bar in the USA. In reality, we were in some kind of abandoned region of Minsk that could have made itself famous in a Zombie movie. This last person that we asked confidently pointed towards a partially open, large metal door that led into one of the construction sites. A man knows he is desperate for some televised sports when he would consider, for even a moment, that going through this door was a remotely good idea. But we were desperate, and in we went.

We carefully walked through the construction site and approached a six-story building that was partially completed. When I say, "partially completed," I mean, the bottom four floors were almost completely unfinished and wide open to the elements, as was the sixth floor. The only apparent floor of the building that could possibly contain a TV was the fifth floor. By this time, it was mid afternoon and we knew the game was about to start. We quickly approached the staircase at the bottom of the building and encountered a really strange sight. There was an old man, of at least 80 years of age, sitting in a small chair at the bottom of the stairs. He had a cane and was smoking a cigarette. This should have been our first warning, but we were not thinking clearly. At this point, all we had on our minds was some food and a soccer game. The old man didn't flinch when we approached him and spent a good three minutes looking us over from the comfort of his little chair. We didn't know what to do, but we got the sense that, somehow, this old man was in charge. He finally took the cigarette out of his mouth and, with a jerk of his head, he motioned for us to pass and go up the stairs.

So up we went. By the time we reached the door to the fifth floor we began to realize that something was really off here. We knocked on the door. A well-dressed bouncer opened the door and stood aside to let us in. What we walked into was a shock to the system. It was like a five-star club and lounge, inclusive of crystal chandeliers, disco lights, a lounge singing act, and a huge sports bar. And yes, there was a TV, and the soccer game was just starting. We hadn't seen anything this nice in months! It was like we had opened a door and stepped into Las Vegas. We sat down and began watching the game. A well-dressed manager approached and introduced himself to us in perfect English. He sat down with us and insisted that we have a round of drinks, on the house. Now this was getting weird and a bit awkward. We started looking around at the dozens and dozens of well-dressed men and wildly dressed women who filled this club, and we realized that this was the local mafia hang out. No one else in Minsk would have been able to afford the food or drinks that were offered here. It was surreal. The lounge singer was singing cover tunes in terribly broken English and the place was just starting to fill up. The manager finally left our table and we began talking together about this odd situation. Our conversation revolved around weighing the wisdom of hanging out with Belarus' most-wanted just so we could watch the soccer game, or getting out of there before something bad happened. Shortly after this conversation our answer arrived in the form of a Belarusian SWAT team.

Even though most day-to-day activities in Eastern Europe were steeped in corruption and mafia activity, there was still a concerted effort by the government to eliminate really significant and threatening criminal elements. As I was looking around the club, I began to notice that at least three-fourths of the people, who had, just minutes before, been partying like there was no tomorrow, suddenly disappeared. Before I could point out this observation to my team mates there was a machine gun pointed right in my face!

Suddenly, there were military-style police, in full-face masks and black body armor, moving quietly through all the tables and rooms in the club. The masked man pointing a gun at me had a small picture clipped to the side of his weapon and was attempting to match our faces to the one he was looking for. The police had quietly and quickly swung in through open windows and had simultaneously entered through all the doors of the premises! They each had pictures clipped to their weapons and they were looking for exact targets. Fortunately, we were not mistaken for the unlucky criminals whose images were etched on those small pictures. Then, as quickly as they had swarmed through the club, they disappeared.

By this time, it was dark outside and the police were gone before I could even get my mind clear enough to realize what had just happened. The police did not find the men they were searching for that day because someone had managed to tip off the most-wanted patrons and they had mysteriously slipped out of the club, seconds before the raid. Then, in no more than five minutes, the club was completely full again and back to business-as-usual, just as before the SWAT team burst in. To this day I have no idea where these people went or how they were tipped off. It was time to go! After this hair-raising experience we decided that no championship soccer game was worth this kind of risk. We quickly exited back down the stairs and headed out of the construction zone.

Chapter 11 ~ The Great Escape!

As soon as we returned from our soccer game extravaganza we discovered that we needed yet another miracle. Upon returning to our hotel, we discovered that there had been a change with the rail system and the train we had planned to take from Minsk to Southern Russia was no longer operating. Sometimes, there is no way to anticipate the types of things that can and will go wrong in our Kingdom assignments. This was a completely unexpected development and our team faced some serious challenges as a result. Each of us had just enough money to purchase the train tickets to Southern Russia. Mike and I had given our team leader the required amount from the money that Mike had borrowed from his bank in England. Although I was penniless at this point, once again, at least I knew I had enough money in the team fund to purchase my anticipated train ticket.

The implications of the altered train schedule began to become clear to us when we learned that there were absolutely no seats available on any other train. This was because Belarusian and Russian citizens had booked up the available space long before, in order to travel to the Black Sea for their summer vacations: the very route we needed to take! Unfortunately, we had no plan-b. We brainstormed together for any kind of alternative plan, but the only alternative we could think of was to obtain super-cheap flights on the insanely dangerous Russian airline, AeroFlot, or, as it was jokingly called in those days, "AeroFlop." At first, there was a glimmer of hope that this might work. However, some people on the team did not feel it was worth the risk to fly this unmaintained airline and one team member's parents flat-out forbade the idea, so we were stuck.

If we could not get to Tuapse, Southern Russia on time, then a cascading domino-effect would begin that would derail our largest camp programs of the summer and, furthermore, would cause Mike and me to miss the flights we had already booked: from Krasnodar to Moscow, then on to Israel, and ultimately back to London. Therefore, if we missed this particular train we would then be stuck indefinitely in Minsk with no money. I hadn't quite envisioned our faith journey ending with Mike and me living on the streets of the former Soviet Union.

Ephesians 6:13 says, *"Therefore, take up the full armor of God, so that you will be able to resist in the evil day, and having done everything, to stand firm."*

Sometimes, when you get to the absolute end of yourself, you can hardly hold your sword up. You feel that you have fought valiantly, persevered, and endured, only to lose the battle within sight of the prize. Paul exhorts us in Ephesians 6:13 *"...having done everything, to stand firm."* There are times in this epic battle when we become so embroiled in the thick of the fight that all we can do is stand our ground.

We were having one of those moments. My teammates and I were battered by a wide range of emotions and responses. Some were angry, especially the guys. Some were so frustrated and upset that weeping was the only response to our circumstances. Mostly it was the girls who cried, and their tears made the guys even more upset about our circumstances. No one likes to feel that they have been defeated in the end, especially not after having seen so many miraculous victories beforehand.

It was the morning on which we had been scheduled to leave by train. The guys got together and decided that we were going to surprise the girls by doing something to cheer them up. Our whole team headed down to market in the morning and while the girls engaged in trinket shopping, the guys assembled all of the nicest foods we could find, and put together a really nice picnic lunch. Little did we know that the subtle hand of the Lord was orchestrating this picnic-shopping plan and that He was about to pull off one of the biggest miracles of the trip!

As we wandered through the market carrying our huge bags of food, we met up with the girls. They were extremely excited and blessed by our genuine attempt to do something nice for them: not a bad effort for a bunch of single guys! Just as we finished explaining our grand plan to the girls, a young Russian boy of no more than ten years old spoke up. By overhearing our conversation in the market the boy had learned of our need for train tickets and that we were literally stuck in Belarus. He approached us and spoke in perfect English saying, "I can get you train tickets." We looked at each other with a mix of humor and amazement. This kid could speak perfect English!

John, our team leader, asked him, "What do you mean, "I can get you train tickets?" The kid said, "I know people," and insisted that he could get us tickets. The bold ten-year-old went on to share that he used to be in the mafia but now he was a Christian and he didn't do that stuff anymore. He said, "All I need you to do is give me your money and all of your passports and I'll have your tickets in less than an hour!"

What? The suggestion that we give this kid our money and passports seemed absolutely crazy and more than a few of our team members spoke against the proposition quite negatively. We were completely thrown off by this situation. Understandably, we were incredulous about the boy's claims. However, as we pressed him a bit more, there actually seemed to be some substance to the boy's assertions. We asked him to hang on a minute while we gathered together for a quick team consultation.

As incredulous as it sounds, we discovered that we were all beginning to actually consider this option. "What do we have to lose?" That was the common thought. "If this kid disappears with our passports and train money we will be in no worse situation than we are right now." But, what a risk! If you are going to be a real asset in the Kingdom of God you have to learn to hear the voice of God. Also, you need to learn how to lead a team to hear the voice of God together. There must be unity and certainty that everyone is hearing the same thing, or these kinds of risks will never even be considered as a possible course of action. I can't overstate the importance of hearing the Lord and obeying in real-time.

Isaiah 30:21 says, *"Your ears will hear a word behind you, 'This is the way, walk in it,' whenever you turn to the right or to the left."*

You can learn to hear the voice of the Lord in any and all circumstances. He is speaking, but often we are not tuned in to hear Him. He may speak through a simple impression in your mind, a vision in your thoughts, by pointing out a scripture to you, or even in an audible voice. The team whose members each learn to hear the Lord independently, and then are encouraged to share what they have heard with each other, becomes convinced of the leading of the Lord because, whatever they have heard personally will be confirmed by the leading that others on the team have heard. This type of listening prayer tunes your spirit in to what the Lord is already saying, so that you can learn to avoid either praying from your own understanding, or offering up powerless maintenance prayers. There is no reason to leave the, "still, small, voice," of the Lord out of your team's prayer process. If you want to find meaning, power and fulfillment in your personal walk with God, then cultivate your spiritual ears to hear and your spiritual eyes to see what the Lord is saying and doing. There is nothing on this earth that compares with living like this. In fact, once you begin to hear the Lord and He begins to know you and trust you with the secrets of His heart, you can't imagine living in any other way.

Our team gathered quickly in the middle of the crowded market to lift this situation before the Lord in prayer and to ask Him to speak to us. We didn't have much time and God didn't need much time. How long does it take for Him to say, "Yes," or, "No?" We went around the group and each person shared what they felt the Lord was saying. It was a unanimous, "Yes." Against all earthly wisdom and better judgement we proceeded to hand over our money and passports to this ten year old who was recently retired from the mafia. As we watched him scamper off through the crowded market we continued to pray, but, honestly, we did not have much faith that this plan would work out. We began walking back to our hotel and were nearly there, when we heard the loud, excited voice of our, little-ex-mafia-train-ticket-kid calling to us, "I got the tickets!" He yelled over and over as he ran toward us. All I could think was, "You have got to be kidding me!"

Since we had not seriously considered the reality that God was going to answer our prayers and work a miracle, we had neglected to prepare in any way for an imminent departure. The ticket kid ran up and handed John all our passports, train tickets and even a receipt! What in the world had just happened? John pressed the kid about how he got the tickets and the kid just said, "I know people. I used to arrange black market tickets all the time!" We realized then that we had better stop asking questions, or we would probably get answers we didn't like. Then the reality of our situation dawned on us. Our train was scheduled to leave in 45 minutes and we hadn't even packed!

We sprinted up to our rooms and scattered in all directions to grab our belongings. There was not even enough time to actually pack our bags, so we scooped up our bags, clothes and toiletries, ran out the front door of the hotel, and threw our belongings into the back of various taxi cabs. "To the train station," we shouted at the drivers, and we were off. This was sight to see: four taxi loads of Americans, speeding and swerving wildly through traffic with people buried under piles of clothes and belongings, frantically stuffing items into backpacks. Each time the taxi took a sharp turn or swerve I went flying across the back seat with clothes and toiletries likewise propelled. It was chaos.

We pulled up to the train station just as our train was beginning to pull out. Our ticket kid had come along with us on the wild taxi ride to make sure we got on the right train, and now he was running at full speed with us toward the departing train. We ran alongside the train and began throwing our bags into any open doors that we could find on various train cars. By the time the last of our team members made the running jump onto the entry ladder, the train was almost traveling too fast to catch at running speed. As we struggled into the hallway of our train car we looked out the window to see our ticket kid sprinting alongside the train. He was waving good bye and yelling, "By the way, don't speak any English on the train!" I yelled back, "Why not?" He replied, "It's a Russians-only train! They'll throw you off!"

I knew something was up with these tickets! As this last-minute communication sunk in, we began to look around to see that we were surrounded by glowering Russian travelers who were not at all pleased to see a bunch of Americans who had somehow been booked into their "Russians-only" train. We slowly slunk back into our bunk rooms and closed the doors. We had to avoid drawing any attention to ourselves if we were to get through even the first border checkpoint without being tossed from this train. The other miracle that had occurred was that, because of our plan to prepare a nice picnic for the girls of our team, we found ourselves prepared with bags of enough food to hold us over for a four-day cross-continent train trip! Not only did we get miraculous train tickets, but also we were provided with food to eat on the journey! There were no other options for purchasing food along the way. It is amazing how the Lord works, quietly making our paths straight and providing for us, even when we are unaware of His working in the background of our lives.

Even though we had comfortable bunk-style beds in this classic 1950's Soviet-era train, we had a hard time sleeping that first night. We were anticipating another Latvian-border-style scenario when we arrived at the first border we were to encounter between Belarus and Ukraine. Once again, the inevitable yelling, fighting and eventual pounding on our train car door ensued. We had arrived at the Ukrainian border. On the Belarusian side of the border the guards checked our tickets, passports and stamped an exit stamp onto our Belarusian visas. They grumbled angrily about how these foreigners had managed to get on this exclusive,

Russians-only train that was headed to the Black Sea. I suspect they were mostly just jealous that they were not on vacation and riding on the party train. The soldiers debated for a few minutes as to whether or not they should toss us off the train or not. They finally waved us back into our train compartment and mumbled something about it being the Ukrainians' problem now. This scenario repeated itself on the Ukrainian side of the border, and then again at the Ukrainian and Russian borders. Each time they found that we were foreigners, the guards would argue and debate about whether it was worth the trouble of tossing us off of the train. They always arrived at the same conclusion: that they should just let us go and we would become the problem of the next set of border guards. God repeatedly intervened to prevent us from ending up in a remote farm field in some part of Eastern Europe. The only thing worse than being a homeless foreigner in a former Soviet city, would be ending up homeless in the middle of nowhere, in a former Soviet republic. Each time the guards waved us through another border, our faith increased and our confidence in the power and ability of our God to "make a way where there seems to be no way," increased dramatically.

In between border crossings, the majority of our four-day train ride to Tuapse passed quietly, and we were actually able to get some rest on the train. However, even though we did our best to ration our picnic food supplies, we began to run low on day three, and became painfully hungry. By the time we arrived in Tuapse, all of us were very ready to be done with train trips for a long time.

Chapter 12 ~ The Watermelon War

The camps we operated in the Tuapse region were both large and challenging. We were to run two camps, of ten days each, with over 100 Russian youth in each program. Facilities at this location were just as bad as at all the other locations where we had held programs over the past three months. Space was severely limited, housing consisted of tight, little, dorm rooms, and bathrooms were the typical, unkept outhouses near the dorms.

Mike and I planned to remain only through to the first few days of the second program, because we had to leave for Moscow and then on to Israel to complete the journey that the Lord had spoken to us about. Although we were saddened that we would miss the second program, we dove full-force into operating the first camp. These were the programs we had spent so much time arranging, and also mobilizing students for, back in the spring when we first arrived in Russia. It was hard to believe that we had begun our adventure for Christ in this very area of Russia, encountering so many difficulties and so many miracles. This field assignment had been so action-packed that it had begun to feel like an entire lifetime. Sometimes I could not even remember what it was like to live anywhere else, and had completely forgotten what it was like to eat good food back in the USA!

The students who came to our program were in various stages of recovery from unbelievably bad childhoods. The majority were in their mid teens, up to about 19 years old. These young people were in the worst condition socially, mentally and spiritually that I had ever encountered. All were from broken homes. This seemed to be the norm. Additionally, most had come through terrible forms of abuse growing up. A world without the knowledge of right and wrong may be the goal of humanist philosophers, but the aftermath and product of that worldview as encountered in Russia, was not a place you would ever want to live. One of the tragic statistics we discovered among our young, female campers was that, on average, almost all the girls had undergone over 12 abortions by the time they were 18 years old! You can imagine the emotional and psychological devastation these precious young girls were suffering from.

During this kind of program it was not uncommon for spiritual bondages to be stirred up inside some of the young people. When this happened, they would begin to manifest demons in various ways. Our first really bad encounter with this dynamic was right in the middle of a worship time during the first camp in Southern Russia. One young girl of about 16 years old began panicking and yelling during the worship service, and then yelled out, "I'm going to Kill Her!" The girl took off at a flat-out run through a dark, dry river bed and most of us guys sprinted after her, not knowing what she, or the spirit in her, intended to do. It was pitch black and we could barely see two feet in front of us as only starlight lit up this rock-filled, dry river bed. We ran with all the speed we could find to try to stop this girl as we realized that she was heading for a huge bridge. There was no doubt in our minds that she intended to jump as soon as she scaled the bridge. One by one, the guys on our team each crashed over rocks in the dark and fell headlong onto the river bed! By God's grace, no one was seriously injured and two of the guys from our team successfully overtook the girl and restrained her from scaling the bridge. After an intense time of prayer and rebuking the evil spirit, she was completely set free that very night! She walked into total freedom and a life-transforming relationship with God during the rest of her camp experience. That is what it is about! We are to take on the wolves and rescue the sheep in the power and by the blood of Jesus Christ! All of our petty physical suffering was put into perspective by the miraculous rescue of this beautiful young girl who needed to be set free from the enemy of her soul. This experience brought me to a new level of understanding as I came to realize that the deliverance and restoration of this young girl was a microcosm of what needed to happen on a national level for Russia and these former Soviet republics. If God can do this for one young person in a remote region of Russia, He can do it on a national scale.

Galatians 5:1 says *"It was for freedom that Christ set us free; therefore keep standing firm and do not be subject again to a yoke of slavery."*

All of mankind longs for freedom and yet so many suffer under a yoke of slavery to sin and the devil. That yoke of slavery is a picture of someone being harnessed like a donkey to pull a cart: a cartload full of sin and condemnation. Praise God that Jesus has raised us up for such works as these. Ephesians 2:10 says, *"For we are His workmanship, created in Christ Jesus for good works, which God prepared beforehand so that we would walk in them."* Don't underestimate what God wants to do, and can do, through you who will listen and obey. Do you want to be noticed by heaven and feared in hell? Do you want to attract the favor of God? If so, let your heart burn with what burns on His heart and do the good works that God has prepared for you! There is absolutely no reason to ever be bored as a follower of Christ. If you are bored, or feel under-challenged or under-utilized in the Kingdom of God, then try to accomplish something that would be impossible if it depended on the strength of men. If the scope of your willingness only allows you to attempt things that are within your experience, educational background or ability to fund, then you are functionally sidelining the power of the Holy Spirit. I believe that it delights the heart of the Lord when we allow ourselves to stretch into areas far beyond our comfort zone and perceived natural abilities in response to His leading. It is almost as if He claps his hands with joy and excitedly leaps toward someone who is willing to do what He wants to do, and trusts Him enough, to completely fall into His empowering arms of Grace. I can see Him saying, "Yes! Here is someone who I can work with and prove myself through!" He is the God who accomplishes above-average things with average people who are yielded to Himself and filled with the Holy Spirit.

In the days leading up to Mike and my departure from the team in order to complete our trip through Moscow, Israel and back to London, there were two impressive moments that stand out in my memory to this day.

There was a girl on our team who I had met in the States during my previous discipleship training program. Her name was Alexis. We had become friends during this eventful faith journey but I never realized until the end of the trip how obedient and faithful to the word of the Lord she was. She had been keeping a secret the whole trip: actually, even longer. During our training programs the previous year God had spoken to her to give me $50; but He had said to her, "Not yet, I'll tell you when it is time." In strict obedience to the Lord, she had not mentioned this to me for over a year, and had held on to this $50 the entire time! Through all of the hardships and needs we had faced, she had refrained from giving me the money out of compassion or human understanding and had waited for the word of the Lord. As the time drew close for Mike and me to depart, I was still in a dire financial situation.

During our journey we received news that an important Christian conference would be happening in Israel at the time we had planned to be there, and that many from our organization planned to attend. Both Mike and I felt that this conference was the purpose of our trip to Israel and that the Lord had something in store for us at this event. We had also learned that the cost to attend this conference, including food and housing, was only $115! Mike had somehow come up with his money, but I was still completely broke! If it had not been for my rations of camp food, I would have had nothing to eat at this point. I'd never been so grateful for food as I was for our regular servings of the fabulous Russian soup called "borscht." I grew to love borscht and still have a fondness for it to this day.

Coming up with $115 in the remaining few days before I reached Israel seemed like a far-fetched possibility. However, I was unmoved in my resolve to see this assignment to its completion, and I was completely confident that somehow the Lord would provide for this last phase of our journey. Shortly before Mike and I were to board the bus back to Krasnodar to catch our flight to Moscow, Alexis came up and handed me $50. She explained the whole story about this $50 to me and I was deeply moved. Not by her generosity really, but by the depth of patience and obedience she had demonstrated by waiting until the Lord told her it was time to give me this money. I thanked her from my heart, and boarded the bus for Krasnodar. I was suddenly $50 closer and only needed $65 dollars more to have enough for this conference.

On the bus ride I began reminiscing about our faith journey and about how we had now come full circle back to Southern Russia. We had literally done the impossible through the power of the One who can make all things possible.

The second event that impacted me strongly that day was witnessing the conclusion of Faith's act of obedience to the Lord. On the plane from London to Krasnodar, Faith had heard from the Lord that she was to pay for Mike and my living expenses up until we reached the first camp in St. Petersburg. Despite our protest, she insisted on providing for us as The Lord had directed, primarily because God had told her He would "repay her 10 times what she spent on us." To her, this was a very good investment and she would not take "no" for an answer! It is a good thing she did not take no for an answer! On the day we were to depart for Moscow, she shared amazing news with us. God had done exactly what He had promised. Faith had spent exactly $100 on us in obedience to the word of the Lord. Now she had just received an unexpected delivery of $1000 to aid her during the year she was to live in Krasnodar! Mike and I were so excited for her that we wanted to do a little victory dance on our crowded bus; but since I was sitting with my legs stretched across open floor boards, with the exposed bus engine roaring directly underneath me, we decided against it.

Our trip to Moscow was mostly uneventful until we reached the city. Moscow in particular was experiencing a season in its history in which, when stepping off of a plane, one felt he had entered the historical, American wild west. In honor of this regular comparison we dubbed it the, "Wild, Wild, East." There were no cowboys or Native Americans, but there were plenty of guns, and everyone was out to get rich quick at any cost.

Mike and I faced an additional layer of risk on this trip because we had been asked to deliver a large amount of money to a network of missionaries in Moscow. There were no ATM's in those days, and other options to obtain currency through a functioning banking system were likewise limited. Of course we agreed to help out, but the level of personal risk we felt was tremendously amplified as we stepped into the wild city of Moscow. At that time, petty mafia, basically street thugs who were adept at spotting a foreigner immediately, prowled the streets. Once spotted, they then planned the foreigner's mugging, or worse. During our many trips on the subway systems we had developed a self-preservation game we called, "Ditch the Mafia." These thugs posed as regular commuters, but then followed a target until he reached an opportune location at which to be relieved of his valuables. Soon we were able to spot these individuals on the crowded subways, because their presence was such a regular occurrence. Our "game" was to sit still when the doors opened, and to not let on that we had reached our stop. The pursuers would nonchalantly stand there, waiting to see if we were getting off. Our tactic was to wait until the final minute before the doors closed, and then suddenly to bolt for the door and exit the train. Usually when the doors closed behind us, the would-be muggers were either automatically stopped, or at least obviously exposed as followers, if they, too, bolted for the closing door. More than once, when a thug moved to pursue us, he then realized we were on to him, and so gave up the chase.

Mike and I employed this tactic multiple times as we entered the subway system and headed for our intended address. When I say "intended" address, that really is the case. Our directions were extremely unclear. We had little idea how to find the apartment at which we were to meet our contacts to deliver their money. The directions we did have went something like this: "Exit the subway at this stop, exit on these stairs, when you come out on the street you'll see a brown building on the right, it's the bottom floor, apartment four, in that building."

This seemed like a reasonable set of instructions until we exited the subway stop as directed and looked out to see not one brown building on the right, but a line of about 20 identical brown buildings on the right! The sun had long since set and it was nearly dark outside. We had just a few remaining minutes of light with which to even glimpse these buildings, much less to determine that they were, in fact, all brown. We began slowly walking toward the buildings as the sky quickly grew completely dark. There were no working street lights and most window curtains were closed, so the darkness felt completely overwhelming. As we walked along a sidewalk mostly by memory and by feeling the way along with our feet, we could hear many people shuffling along in all directions around us. It was like being in a creepy zombie movie! We were trying our best to fit into the type of walking and shuffling along that everyone else was doing, in order to avoid drawing attention to ourselves. Suddenly, there was a burst of gunfire not 20 feet away from us. The sound was deafening and the flash quickly lit up the street scene, revealing dozens of eerie figures who were standing still like statues all around us. We, too, froze in place for a split second after the gunfire. Then, as if nothing had happened, everyone began moving along in their various directions again. "We have got to get off the street!" Mike whispered in my ear. If someone targeted us it would be as if they had won the lottery, with all the cash we were carrying!

As we approached the line of buildings, all we could do was stop for a second or two and quickly pray, asking God to tell us which building it was. With so much dangerous and unpredictable activity going on all around us in the dark, we might not get a second chance to choose a building. We both immediately heard the same thing from the Lord, "Choose the fourth building on the right." We headed there immediately, as fast as we could walk without drawing attention to ourselves in the dark. Finding the door for apartment number four was also not easy without light to see by.

We found what we believed was the correct door and knocked lightly. "Who is it?" someone yelled in a whisper through the door. When we gave our names and told them who had sent us, they opened the door right away. Mike and I were both grabbed by the arms at the same time, and pulled headlong, over an upside-down couch that was obviously positioned to reinforce the door. We landed in a pile on the floor and the older missionary couple, who were well into their 60's said, "Welcome to Moscow!" What had we gotten ourselves into?

"Stay low and don't let your shadow form a silhouette against the window curtains," the missionary said. "Why?" I asked, "What is going on?" "Don't you know?" he said. "We are in the middle of a massive turf war between two large, rival mafia factions and they are massacring each other over who has the right to sell watermelons!" He went on to explain that this "watermelon war," as it had been locally referred to, was in a stalemate at the moment, but most of the fighting had been in the open field just behind their row of buildings. These factions were using such heavy-duty weapons and in such a protracted conflict that our missionary hosts were convinced there had been some kind of coup in Russia. They finally were able to place a call to a local TV station on the day before we arrived and were greatly relieved that there had not been a coup, and that this mini war was only about watermelon sales. So here we were, overnighting at an apartment that we were not able to even walk around in. We had to stay low all night, eat sitting on the floor, and sleep on the floor, to avoid making ourselves a target for snipers. Bullets had come through this couple's windows on occasion already, so the house rules were not without reason. Mike and I gratefully accepted their hospitality and spent the evening telling them news about other contacts they knew around Russia. Then we spent some time in prayer and worship together. They were a sweet and dedicated couple, and I had become friends with their daughter who lived briefly at the missions training center in Oregon.

In the morning, Mike and I slipped out of the apartment just before dawn, to catch the first subway train back to the airport. At this time of morning, most of the local combatants were either too drunk or hung over to carry on fighting, and so it was much safer to move around.

Chapter 13 ~ Onward to Israel

We arrived in Tel Aviv without incident. This was my first time in Israel and also my first time in the Middle East. What a change of environment from the last four months in the former Soviet Union! Being back in a first-world country put me into reverse culture shock. One of the oddest things that I distinctly remember about arriving at the airport in Tel Aviv, was the way my eyes were overwhelmed by the bright lights and colors, particularly of average signs. I had not seen brightly lit colors and signs for so long that it actually overwhelmed my senses for the first few days. The abundance of food also contributed to my culture shock. It was everywhere. You might think I had never lived in a first-world nation up until that moment. When one has been deeply immersed in such a stressful foreign environment for a long period of time, one forgets much of who he is. The only down side to the abundance of food was that I could not afford to buy any of it! I was completely focused on saving my $50 toward the conference fees, but I also had to live for a few days in Jerusalem before the conference began. By God's grace, a local Christian worker housed and fed us for the first few days we were there, so I didn't have to spend money from my carefully saved $50.

After acclimating a bit to our new culture and environment, we decided to venture out to the popular Jerusalem hang-out street called, "Ben Yahuda." This street is lined with restaurants, clubs and shops. It is the center of night life for much of Jerusalem. Thousands of people crowd this street every evening and I was about to realize that nothing can hide you from God's blessing, even in a massive crowd.

As we walked along this crowded street in the early evening, I began to hear someone call my name. I kept looking around, but did not see anyone. Finally, I spotted a blonde head of hair coming my direction through the ocean of people. A young woman suddenly appeared right in front of me and yelled out over the crowd noise, "There you are!"

"Here I am!" I yelled back. At first I did not realize who it was, but I soon recognized that this woman had participated in my discipleship program in Oregon during the previous year. "What are you doing here?" I asked loudly, over the noise of the partying crowd. "Looking for you!" She said. I was confused. "How did you know I would be here?" I asked. She replied, "God told me that I would find you down on Ben Yahuda street tonight, and told me that I was supposed to give you $65, do you need money for something?" I was floored. Not too much, not too little, and never too late: this was the hand of the Lord, and He was making the point that He was leading and He was providing.

We moved out of the loud area of the street and sat down to visit at a cafe. I explained to her that, Yes, I needed exactly $65 in order to have enough to attend the conference I had registered for here in Israel. She handed me the money and said, "I'm here for the same conference." God had drawn a number of His people to this event. Again, I was so impressed by the absolute trust in the voice of the Lord that this woman, and also the women on my team in Russia, had demonstrated. True confidence in the Lord caused the women to become powerful in their obedience.

God does not begin His personal communication and interaction with most of us by asking us to take a nation. He often starts out asking us small, simple, and personal questions, and gives us very easy instructions and suggestions to follow. As we begin to act in obedience and agreement with the Lord on small things, He increasingly begins to build our confidence and trust in Himself by asking us to do increasingly harder and more significant things. Quite often we find that we miss the still, small, voice of the Lord, even on the simple things, but the art of relationship is that you keep trying to hear and obey. Often now, I find that it's the small whispers in my spirit about seemingly insignificant things that turn out to be the voice of the Lord, and if I heed those quiet words in my spirit, I will be spared many mistakes and losses in life. It is truly a walk with the Lord and, just like all relationships, it takes time and intentional cultivation to develop a trusting and close relationship with God. Once you do, you find that this is the absolute meaning of life. There is nothing more awe-inspiring, rewarding and life-giving than to have the creator of the universe not only lead you in the simple things in life, but also share the secrets of His heart with you! The bible says in Psalms 25:14 *"The secret of the Lord is for those who fear Him, And He will make them know His covenant."*

I can honestly say that this type of walk with God is available to anyone who will seek Him out. If I, and many other average followers of Jesus, can cultivate this kind of relationship with Him, then you can do it as well. Don't give in to the inner feelings of inadequacy that plague us all. Don't let the deceiver tell you that you have to be special, educated, perfectly behaved, or any other lie. None of this is true. Often I have found that the people who have the most enviable relationships with God are those who pursue a simple and deep, personal love relationship with their Heavenly Father. Ultimately, nothing else matters but this epic pursuit.

Chapter 14 ~ Five Dollars

Mike and I attended the conference as planned. Before the first day of the conference was over, the Lord's reason for so strongly directing us to participate became clear. The nexus of speaking topics focused significant emphasis on the recent immigration of thousands of Eastern European Jews to Israel. These immigrants were uprooted Russians and Ukrainians, etc., who suddenly found themselves relocated in Israel, but were still very much defined by their home cultures. During the course of the event God gave me clear instructions and a vision to return to Israel in the future to organize discipleship youth programs similar to those we had recently conducted in the former Soviet Union.

Sometimes you don't find out the "why" of a situation until after you obey. If you find yourself continually questioning the Lord about His leading in your life, demanding to know the details and to know "why," you will silence that still, small, voice in your heart. How does the verse from the old hymn go? "Trust and obey, for there is no other way, to be happy in Jesus, but to trust and obey." When our first response to the quiet leading of the Lord is to pepper Him with questions and clarifications it often is a sign that we do not actually trust Him. Not trusting the Lord is an indictment of His character. When we sense the leading of the Lord and we question or reason against it we are often saying in our hearts, "I don't believe that You have my highest and best in mind and I'm not going to do this until I'm convinced that you are actually good, loving and trustworthy." Relating to God in this way will not produce a deep and loving closeness in which the Lord will share the secrets of His heart with you. Do you want to know what God thinks? Do you want to become familiar with the "ways" of God? Then trust and obey. Trust that He is who He says He is in His word, and trust Him in the small things so that He can entrust you with the large things in His world.

Mike and I packed up our few belongings and headed back to England after the conference was over. Once again, I was completely broke and was grateful to be able to hitch a ride with a van load of people going from the conference to the airport in Tel Aviv. Now, I was a sight to see at this point in my journey. I had long surfer hair that had grown down to my shoulders and my clothes were ragged and worn out. The only shoes I had were an old pair of hiking boots that I had miraculously found in a market in Russia after my first pair of boots wore out. I looked a lot like a stereotypical homeless guy. I had learned over the years that this kind of appearance does not win any favors when going through customs and security in airports. Therefore, our strategy was to to bring along one pair of dress pants and a dress shirt, to be reserved only for traveling in and out of western airports. When I was in Russia, no one even noticed or cared what I looked like, but this was not the case in Israel and England. So we did our best to get dressed up and make ourselves presentable.

We passed through security at the airport and found our way to our boarding gate. I was adjusting my carry-on and looking for something in my pockets when suddenly, in the front left pocket of my dress pants I came across a folded up $5 bill. Now, I hadn't worn these pants since we left the USA over four months ago and I had never thought to check these pockets over the past four months! As I pulled out the $5 bill and carefully unfolded it the Lord clearly spoke to me and said, "See, you didn't even need the money that you had." When I left the USA this was all the money I had on hand to last me through the entire four month assignment! God made it clear to me that when I was acting in complete obedience and trust, I didn't even need this.

I just about jumped up and down as I showed Mike my discovery and told him what the Lord had said. "What are you going to do with it?" Mike asked. It was as if we had found a bar of Gold instead of $5. "I don't know," I said. This $5 had taken on kind of a mystical significance in light of the experiences of the last four months.

After a graciously uneventful flight back to London we arrived at Heathrow airport and called Mike's mom for a ride. All I could think about was that I loved coffee and we had been mostly coffee-deprived during the past four months, due either to general lack of availability or lack of money. So while we waited for Mike's mom to arrive and take us to their home in Ipswich, Mike and I found a small, airport cafe, and used the $5 to buy two cups of coffee.

What a life-altering adventure! This experience changed everything. I have never again been satisfied with anything average in my walk with God. I knew that God had taken me on this assignment to test my trust in Him and to build foundations for many adventures that were to come. One of the most distinct changes I saw in myself became apparent while at Mike's home in Ipswich. One day, five of his older brother's friends from University cornered me in the living room. They had heard about the nature of our trip and they knew of our faith in God. These students were atheists studying at top universities in England. Not only were they hostile to Christianity but they also wanted to drag me into a debate about philosophy to attempt to disprove my "notions" of God. I did not have answers at that time in my life for all of their philosophical contentions, so when they confronted me, demanding that I somehow "prove" the existence of God, I found myself overcoming by the 'word of my testimony'.

This was the first time that I suddenly found myself sharing this very story in unified detail. These young men who were initially argumentative and arrogant, sat with their mouths literally hanging open as I shared for over half of an hour. When I was done they looked around at each other in disbelief and shock. One of them finally spoke up and said, "Well, obviously it works for you." That was the last time they tried to talk to me about "religion." This was also where I realized the power and truth of what the Bible talks about when it says, *"And they overcame him because of the blood of the Lamb and because of the word of their testimony, and they did not love their life even when faced with death."* (Revelation 12:11)

If you don't have a testimony then get one! Ask God to lead you into the waters of impossibility to do something that cannot be done unless God does it through you. Don't settle for anything less in life.

www.ingramcontent.com/pod-product-compliance
Lightning Source LLC
Chambersburg PA
CBHW051950290426
44110CB00015B/2184